POWER
ENGAGE

SEVEN POWER
MOVES FOR
BUILDING STRONG
RELATIONSHIPS
TO INCREASE
ENGAGEMENT
WITH STUDENTS
AND PARENTS

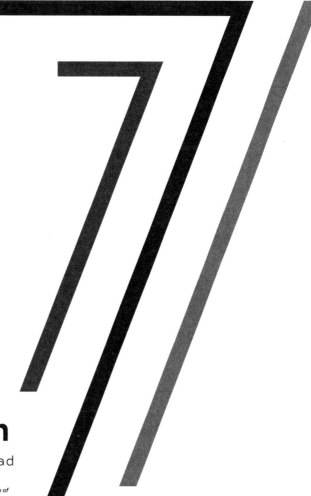

Carlos Johnson

Foreword by Anthony Muhammad

Solution Tree | Press

a division of
Solution Tree

555 North Morton Street
Bloomington, IN 47404
800.733.6786 (toll free) / 812.336.7700
FAX: 812.336.7790

email: info@SolutionTree.com
SolutionTree.com

Visit **go.SolutionTree.com/studentengagement** to download the free reproducibles in this book.

Printed in the United States of America

Library of Congress Cataloging-in-Publication Data

Names: Johnson, Carlos (Educational consultant), author.
Title: Power engage : seven moves for building strong relationships to
  increase engagement with students and parents / Carlos Johnson.
Description: Bloomington, IN : Solution Tree Press, [2024] | Includes
  bibliographical references and index.
Identifiers: LCCN 2023022830 (print) | LCCN 2023022831 (ebook) | ISBN
  9781954631694 (paperback) | ISBN 9781954631700 (ebook)
Subjects: LCSH: Teacher-student relationships--United States. |
  Teaching--Methodology. | Parent-teacher relationships--United States. |
  Home and school--United States.
Classification: LCC LB1033 .J56 2024 (print) | LCC LB1033 (ebook) | DDC
  371.102/30973--dc23/eng/20230814
LC record available at https://lccn.loc.gov/2023022830
LC ebook record available at https://lccn.loc.gov/2023022831

Solution Tree
Jeffrey C. Jones, CEO
Edmund M. Ackerman, President

Solution Tree Press
President and Publisher: Douglas M. Rife
Associate Publishers: Todd Brakke and Kendra Slayton
Editorial Director: Laurel Hecker
Art Director: Rian Anderson
Copy Chief: Jessi Finn
Senior Production Editor: Sarah Foster
Copy Editor: Madonna Evans
Proofreader: Charlotte Jones
Text and Cover Designer: Laura Cox
Acquisitions Editor: Hilary Goff
Assistant Acquisitions Editor: Elijah Oates
Content Development Specialist: Amy Rubenstein
Associate Editor: Sarah Ludwig
Editorial Assistant: Anne Marie Watkins

This book is dedicated to all those who taught me and pushed me.

To those who sheltered me while I researched and wrote my third book. To those who shaped me through education, such as my math teacher, Ms. Hunter, who taught me that everything adds up in life. To my wrestling coaches, Twin and Shep, who taught me to never give up.

And to those who hugged, trained, encouraged, and inspired me, such as my close friends Anthony Muhammad, Principal Kafelle, Ken Williams, Chris Martin, and my coach, Ian Watts.

Finally, to those who loved me with care and correction: my parents, Bernice and Arnold Brandon, who lovingly taught me the consequences of being right and wrong.

Even though they all had different roles, their collective input amounted to one great push!

Therefore, it is with these people in mind that I quote my track coach, James Horton:

*"If you cannot win the race,
push
the man in front of you so that
he breaks the world record."*

Acknowledgments

Solution Tree Press would like to thank the following reviewers:

Doug Crowley
Assistant Principal
DeForest Area High School
DeForest, Wisconsin

Ann Delehant
Consultant
Learning Forward
Webster, NY

Chad Dumas
Educational Consultant
Next Learning Solutions
Ames, Iowa

John D. Ewald
Education Consultant
Frederick, Maryland

Salvador Herrera
Principal
Robertson Continuation High School
Fremont, CA

Laura Hesson
Washington County School District
Board Member
Washington County School District
St. George, Utah

Janet Gilbert
Principal
Mountain Shadows Elementary
School
Glendale, Arizona

Agnes Miller
Test Coordinator and Academic Dean
Charlotte, North Carolina

Keri Rathbun
Principal
Northside High School
Fort Smith, AR

Jose "JoJo" Reyes
Chief Administration Officer
Parlier Unified School District
Parlier, California

Katie Saunders
Middle Level Teacher
Anglophone School District West
Woodstock, New Brunswick

Kory Taylor
Reading Interventionist
Arkansas Virtual Academy
Little Rock, Arkansas

James E. Spruill
Owner
Urban Divide Technology
Inkster, Michigan

Ringnolda Jofee' Tremain
K–8 Principal
Trinity Leadership Arlington
Arlington, Texas

Rachel Swearengin
Fifth-Grade Teacher
Manchester Park Elementary School
Olathe, Kansas

Visit **go.SolutionTree.com/studentengagement** to download the free reproducibles in this book.

Table of Contents

Reproducibles are in italics.

About the Author

 **Coach Carlos Johnson** is a professional speaker, trainer, author, and school administrator. For roughly twenty years, he has consulted, trained, and held seats on public, charter, and private school boards.

Along with his team of consultants at IMAGE of Success, Coach Carlos uses many of Anthony Muhammad's (2018) philosophies from *Transforming School Culture: How to Overcome Staff Division*. He has successfully turned around three failing schools simply by concentrating on the school's culture and the school-home relationship. His particular focus is on the idea that instructional teams are not only the delivery system for high-quality instruction. Their relationships with students and families can also drive or destroy school culture and performance.

The research and results from this philosophy led him to create his systematic approach to building healthy performance-based relationships with all stakeholders. He calls this system *PowerEngage*. In addition to working with district leaders and instructional teams, Coach Carlos's online parent training at PowerParentingU. com helps hundreds of parents each year become certified Partner Parents by training them on what he calls the seven meaningful minimum strategies for engaging with their child's school. As head of school, he led the Male Leadership Academy in Charlotte, North Carolina, to consistent increases in enrollment, and his parental promise of at least one year's growth for one year's attendance was met each year for 100 percent of his students.

To book Carlos Johnson for professional development, contact pd@ SolutionTree.com.

Foreword

by Anthony Muhammad

I grew up in the midwestern industrial town of Flint, Michigan, in the 1970s during the so-called golden age of American industrialism. Nearly every adult I knew worked for General Motors. There were abundant manufacturing opportunities, so most people had labor opportunities and earned good wages.

This reality created a very specific culture in my school system. The prevailing mentality was that Flint would always be an industrial giant, and school was a place to house students and keep them safe until they dropped out of high school and worked in the factories or graduated and worked in the factories. The foregone conclusion was that school was not a place to help shape a young person's future; school was a place to prepare students for a predetermined future in manufacturing. Consequently, I did not have a joyful experience in the K–12 system. Our teachers were more concerned about compliance than enlightenment and about order than engagement. The best way to describe my school experience is that I felt more like a hostage than a student.

In the 1980s, American automotive factories began to close. Foreign competition and the impact of automation made factory workers less desirable. The prevailing assumption that simple attendance and compliance were the gateways to a prosperous future became obsolete nearly overnight. My hometown offered more than 100,000 automotive manufacturing jobs at its peak, a number that had fallen to less than 10,000 by the year 2000. The once-proud city is a sad caricature of its former glory.

Fortunately, with the support of my mother and a few very dynamic teachers, I avoided the tragedy of unemployment and poverty that many experienced after the fall of the auto industry. I graduated college and graduate school, and I have a thriving career. I leaned on my support system to avoid the pitfalls of an education that did not value, build, or promote student engagement. Unfortunately, many of my peers did not have that same support system and suffered deeply because of it. Why did my school system serve us like that? Was there a way that they could have made the experience joyful and beneficial? Could they have engaged us, our parents, and our community in a way that would have helped many of my peers navigate the tremendous downturn in the city's economic future? Of course, they could have—they just chose not to.

I first met Carlos Johnson in 2002 when I was a principal at Levey Middle School in Southfield, Michigan. Carlos was not a teacher but a concerned citizen and entrepreneur who did work within a school system and used his knowledge, skills, and resources to support schools. Carlos was the ultimate advocate! We became close friends, and Carlos partnered with me to help serve some of the neediest students in my school. What struck me most about Carlos was his sincere concern for student well-being and success.

I see this book as the culmination of Carlos's growth as a man, a professional, and a champion for children. The beauty of this book is that it provides educators with research, evidence, tools, and resources to create a unified approach to lighting the fire within every child. After reading this book, I thought about how different my school experience in Flint could have been if educators had read this book in the 1970s.

It is too late for me to go back and revisit my childhood school experience, but it is not too late for you to bless your students today with what we were denied as students. It is not good enough to simply say, "We've always done it this way." The times are too serious, and student needs are too diverse. We live in a society where automation, artificial intelligence, and innovation make student skills, critical thinking, and emotional intelligence paramount if students hope to have a bright future.

Carlos has provided the reader with a framework to understand engagement and tools to promote engagement. What I like most about this book is that Carlos places his greatest premium on the development of the child and calls on us to collaborate to implement the strategies that can help each child blossom. I understand that, at the time of this writing, many of us are still recovering physically and emotionally from the stain of a global pandemic. Parents and students are still recovering from the impact, as well. Many things in our current reality might make us go into psychological flight. We are all tired! But, if we don't emerge from this tragedy with a renewed sense of commitment, vigor, and professionalism, we risk losing an entire generation as we did with deindustrialization in the 1980s.

In conclusion, I implore you to not only read this book but also think about its utility within our current challenges. If we do not learn from the past, we will repeat it. In 2023, students should not feel like hostages. They deserve classrooms and school cultures that bring out their best attributes and adults who are passionate about their future and are willing to change their practices on students' behalf. Now is not the time to lie down; now is the time to engage at every level!

Anthony Muhammad, PhD, is a much sought-after educational speaker and presenter. A practitioner for nearly twenty years, he has served as a middle school teacher, assistant principal, and principal, and as a high school principal. His Transforming School Culture approach explores the root causes of staff resistance to change.

Sound The Alarm:
Students Must Engage

One if by land, and two if by sea;
And I on the opposite shore will be,
Ready to ride and spread the alarm
Through every Middlesex village and farm,
For the country folk to be up and to arm.

—Henry Wadsworth Longfellow

The excerpt from "Paul Revere's Ride" (Longfellow, 1860) describes how Paul Revere sounded the alarm during the American Revolutionary War. Now, in the United States, our teachers, students, and educational systems are at risk, and it's time to sound the alarm again. With this book, I want to sound that alarm and provide tools for teachers looking for solutions they can implement right now. They need proven solutions that don't always require budget or central office approval.

I also sound the alarm because a well-educated workforce is a key part of a successful society, which makes education a prerequisite for economic prosperity. Why do I say that? Because major findings by the Economic Policy Institute (Berger & Fisher, 2013) include the following data.

- A clear and strong correlation exists between the educational attainment of a state's workforce and median wages in the state.

- States can build a strong foundation for economic success and shared prosperity by investing in education.

- Expanded access to high-quality education will not only expand economic opportunity for residents, but also likely do more to strengthen the overall state economy than anything else a state government can do.

If that's not enough to sound the alarm, how about this: according to the Pew Research Center (2016), physical or manual skills—in demand some three decades ago—are fading in importance. Further, a well-trained teacher is likely to send more students to college and can boost a class's lifetime income by $250,000 (Chetty, Friedman, & Rockoff, 2014). Even if college is not a student's priority, a well-trained teacher inspires students to achieve in and out of the classroom.

An uneducated workforce threatens us all, which means we can't afford for too many of our students to become disengaged or drop out of school. We must intervene. We must sound the alarm.

Sounding the alarm is an important first step, but it is not enough. We must also offer solutions, and that's why *Power Engage* provides seven research-based and field-tested power moves. Since we have written and rewritten curriculum, promised to leave No Child Left Behind, and ensured that Every Student Succeeds, let's address one of our biggest opportunities to help students succeed. Let's endeavor to create a classroom and school culture that commits to building healthy relationships that drive student engagement in *every* student in *every* classroom.

I have found that student disengagement not only makes teaching difficult but also sabotages the hopes and dreams of many families, schools, and districts. Yes, we've made strides, and often we have been successful; but if we are honest, there's more to do. For now, let's take our energy level and work even smarter, not harder. We can't get weary now.

This book aims to sound the alarm about the importance of the teacher-student relationship just as Anthony Muhammad (2018) sounded the alarm regarding staff division in his book *Transforming School Culture: How to Overcome Staff Division*, as Gary Keller and Jay Papasan (2013) did in their book *The ONE Thing: The Surprisingly Simple Truth Behind Extraordinary Results*, and as Richard DuFour and Robert Eaker (1998) sounded the alarm for schools to transform by becoming professional learning communities (PLCs) in their seminal work *Professional Learning Communities at Work®: Best Practices for Enhancing Student Achievement.*

Sound the Alarm! Students Must Engage!

If the **school** is the place where teachers and students are always supposed to be safe,

Somebody had better sound the alarm because the **school** is under attack!

Sound the alarm because Michelle's parents can't help her read because they can't read.

Sound the alarm because Michael learned he has ADD before he learned to add.

Sound the alarm because one school receives $4,000 per child, and another receives $14,000 per child, but both schools have the same learning expectations.

Sound the alarm because too many students can't pass a drug test.

Sound the alarm because twelve million children live in poverty.

Sound the alarm because for too many students their address and not their intelligence determines their success.

Sound the alarm because our sons have turned underwear into outerwear.

Sound the alarm because to our young daughters, Victoria's Secret is no longer a secret.

Sound the alarm because our jails and courtrooms are filled with young men who should be in our classrooms!

Sound the alarm because too many of our daughters go from dressing **Barbies to burping babies**.

Sound the alarm because there was a time when most parents would say, "NO! because I said so, and that is the end of discussion," and now too often young people yell, "I hate you," and that is the **end of the discussion**.

Sound the alarm because there was a time when schools and parents were united from the time kids got on the bus. Now too often, it's THEM versus US!

Sound the alarm because it is wartime,

and

Woe be it to the school leader, teacher, or parent who acts the same way in WARtime as they do in PEACEtime.

Sound the alarm from every living room, classroom, and stage.

Sound the alarm because students must engage!

Introduction

> Give me a lever long enough, and a fulcrum on which to place it, and
> I shall move the world.
>
> —Archimedes

Each school day in the United States, approximately 54.4 million students attend preK–12 public and private schools (National Center for Education Statistics, n.d.). Additionally, approximately 5.7 million students attend preK–12 public and private schools in Canada (Statistics Canada, 2021). Not one of these students can learn if they are not engaged in the process of learning.

If your goal is to increase the level of student engagement in the learning process, then this book is for you. While there are many credible definitions for *student engagement*, I have found this one to sum it up the best: "Student engagement refers to the degree of attention, curiosity, interest, value, and perseverance that students show when they are learning or being taught" (Olson & Peterson, 2015, p. 1).

To help you achieve your goal, this book provides research and practice for building what I call *performance-based relationships*, which are the caring connections built between students and families when educators implement learning and behavior expectations with equitable compassion and accountability. As shown in figure I.1 (page 2), compared to other kinds of teacher-student relationships, performance-based relationships create the most engagement.

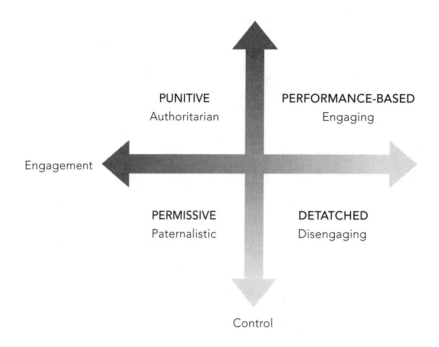

PUNITIVE Authoritarian	**PERFORMANCE-BASED** Engaging
PERMISSIVE Paternalistic	**DETATCHED** Disengaging

Engagement

Control

Figure I.1: Teacher-student relationships matrix.

Understanding Performance-Based Relationships

The term *relationship* can frighten many people because of their past experiences and because the term can be ambiguous. The New Oxford American Dictionary defines *relationship* (2015) as "the way in which two or more concepts, objects, or people are connected." The primary way in which students and their families connect to teachers is through academic performance. Hence, my term *performance-based relationships*.

> **POWER**IDEA
>
> *Performance-based relationships* are the caring connections built between students and families when educators implement learning and behavior expectations with equitable compassion and accountability.

The term *performance-based relationships* reminds us of the purpose of our interactions and relationships with students. Yes, we want to build healthy, inspiring relationships, but we are not our students' best friends or their extended family. We ground our relationships with students in the hopes that they will learn and then leave us to become their best selves possible.

The term *performance-based relationships* also reminds us that we have no or very little ability to alter certain student status variables, while other student status variables are more in our control. Distinguishing between variables that are in or out of our control is important because it sets teachers up to operate in a safe place during self-reflection and performance evaluation. Table I.1 provides lists of variables that we can and cannot control.

Table I.1: Status Variables

Status Variables Out of Our Control	Status Variables Within Our Control
Student's socioeconomic status and home environment	Orderly classroom environment
Students' parents' relationship status	Compassionate accountability
Spiritual beliefs	Interactive curriculum
Sexual orientation	Equitable discipline policies
Dietary choices	Culturally responsive teaching

The purpose of our relationships with students and their families is to improve student achievement. Therefore, during the time we have our students, our primary goal should be to build the type of relationships that foster trust and motivate students to positively engage both academically and behaviorally.

Building these relationships is the perfect work for classroom teachers and building leaders from preK to college who serve students and their families, who are often discouraged and disengaged from the learning process. Performance-based relationships are good for all students; however, a healthy teacher-student relationship is life changing for a student who is discouraged, disengaged, or headed for destruction.

Targeting Student Groups

When I work with school districts to assess teacher-student relationships, student engagement, and school culture, I use the school's data and divide students into three subgroups.

1. *Engaged students* are the school's fully engaged highflyers. Let's be clear, membership in this group is not about genetics—it's about guidance. These students often have an excellent support network that provides them with one or all of the following: a life vision, direction, structure, role models, healthy consequences, and resources. Thus, they arrive at school well-fed, focused, and fired up to engage!

2. *Partially engaged students* have just enough engagement to pass their classes but not enough interest or motivation to become a member of

the high achievers club. They exist in that space between survival and suspension, and everyone knows they have more potential than what they demonstrate. These students are engaged just enough to get by but not enough to excel in school.

3. *Disengaged students* have not found the engagement on-ramp to learning or maybe even the on-ramp to student culture. Additionally, they may not have found their champion teachers to connect to. Their family lives are likely a constant economic and environmental struggle. Because of their lack of success economically, socially, and academically, they carry little joy or hope and often demonstrate behavioral problems. For many reasons, they don't believe they belong in class or school. They represent the most disengaged students.

Table I.2 summarizes each of the three groups.

Table I.2: Features of Student Groups

Student Group	Group Features
Engaged students	Engaged students are the school's fully engaged highflyers. Membership is not about genetics; it's about support and guidance. Students arrive well-fed, focused, and fired up to engage.
Partially engaged students	Partially engaged students have just enough engagement to pass their classes, but not enough interest or motivation to become a member of the highflyers club.
Disengaged students	Disengaged students are fully disengaged, socially and academically. They may not have found their champion teachers to connect to. Their family lives are a constant struggle economically and environmentally. For many reasons, they don't believe they belong in class or school.
Note: Due to many variables, these designations are a framework and not meant to pigeonhole any student or determine future performance.	

The research on connective instruction by researcher Kristy Cooper (2013) indicates that healthy teacher-student relationships are seven times more effective than academic rigor. Why? Because students have a desperate need for high-quality relationships. When a teacher fulfills that desire, student achievement and intellectual functioning soar. If you realize that your content mastery alone is not enough to help the partially engaged and disengaged students and want to find ways to increase their engagement, this book is for you.

Discovering What's in This Book

Can I interest you in a KISS (keep it simple system)? What if I told you that simple could also be effective? The mathematician Archimedes told us that even the most difficult task can have a simple and effective solution (Encyclopedia. com, n.d.).

To make your life simpler, each chapter includes important tips called *power ideas*. These power ideas are for easy reference when looking for tips or morning motivation. In addition, this book has two parts for easy reference and usability.

Part 1, Inspiration and Foundation, provides the inspiration and information needed to realize the power to transform your classroom culture and students' performance.

- Chapter 1: Discover the One Thing That Can Change Everything
- Chapter 2: Get Our Buts Out of the Way—Relationship Mindsets

Part 2, Implementation, presents seven research-based and field-tested strategies to help you accomplish one very important goal: increase student relationships so you can increase student engagement. I call the following seven strategies *power moves*, which we explore in chapters 3–9.

- Chapter 3: Power Move—Adopt the Classroom Coach Mindset
- Chapter 4: Power Move—Know Your *High Why* for Teaching
- Chapter 5: Power Move—Help Students Find Their *High Why*
- Chapter 6: Power Move—Foster Cooperative Competition
- Chapter 7: Power Move—Educate and Celebrate Parents as Partners
- Chapter 8: Power Move—Target Your Boys
- Chapter 9: Power Move—Measure Student Engagement Frequently

As we discuss in chapters 3 and 4, the first two power moves are reflective and aspirational strategies for your own self-care and personal growth. These strategies are the engines and fuel for the five power moves discussed in chapters 5–9. These power moves are classroom strategies for transforming your classroom through increased healthy engagement with students and their families. Each power move provides at least one tool for review, reflection, and implementation. Chapter 10 discusses the engagement evidence chain to help you ensure that the strategies in this book are working in your classroom. After reading this book, you will have twelve unique relationship-building and engagement power move tools for easy and instant application.

Educators can implement all seven power moves together or individually while maintaining their effectiveness. None of the power moves are dependent on the other. Simply implement as needed in your classroom or as a grade-level or school-wide initiative. Most importantly, these power moves, for the most part, are entirely within the individual teacher's control, and most do not need district funding or approval. At the end of the book, on page 113, you'll find a reproducible chart that can help you determine which power move would be most beneficial at any given time depending on your current situation and needs.

Finally, you can work through this book alone or read it with others to enhance team skills. If you are a building leader, you can lead your instructional team through the implementation of one power move per month or perhaps have different teams try different power moves and then share their experiences. When implemented with fidelity, efficacy, and sincerity, these power moves become your Archimedes levers that, placed in the right school fulcrum, can transform the culture of a grade level or the entire school.

PART 1

Inspiration
and Foundation

CHAPTER 1

Discover the One Thing That Can Change Everything

Both research and practice offer one inescapable, insightful conclusion to those considering an improvement initiative: change is difficult.

—Richard DuFour

While change can be difficult, the most important step toward change is the first one. As a child growing up in Michigan, the winters were brutal, but they were also fun. I still have vivid memories of snowball fights and the day my dad taught me how to make a snowman. He showed me that all I needed to start was to make a small snowball and then roll it over and over into the snow until it was a bigger ball. I repeated the process three times, one for the snowman's lower body, one for the midsection, and finally, one for the snowman's head. But the snowman started with the first small snowball. Little did I know that my dad was also teaching me the domino effect.

This chapter discusses the domino effect and how it can start a cascade of improvements in classrooms and schools. The power moves described in chapters three and four will offer ideas for starting this cascade. Later in this chapter, we look at the importance of caring human relationships. Finally, we look at the effect size of building relationships with students.

Understanding the Domino Effect

A study by the University of British Columbia physicist Lorne Whitehead (1983) demonstrates the *domino effect*: when you knock over a single domino, it can knock over a subsequent domino that is approximately one and a half times larger. University of Toronto professor Stephen Morris (2009) used this theory to show that if you lined up twenty-nine progressively larger dominos, with the first domino being five millimeters (the size of a pencil eraser), the twenty-ninth and last one could wipe out the Empire State Building.

The domino effect impacts our personal lives. In 2012, a group of researchers at the Northwestern University Feinberg School of Medicine wanted to figure out the most effective way to spur people to change common bad health habits, such as eating too much saturated fat and not enough fruits and vegetables, spending too much time in sedentary leisure, and not getting enough physical activity. The study found that when people decreased their sedentary leisure time each day, they also reduced their fat intake. The researchers never told participants to eat less fat, but their nutrition habits improved as a natural side effect of spending less time on the couch watching television and mindlessly eating (Northwestern University Feinberg School of Medicine, 2012). In other words, one habit led to another; or, one domino knocked down the next.

In *The ONE Thing: The Surprisingly Simple Truth Behind Extraordinary Results*, real estate executives Gary Keller and Jay Papasan (2013) describe achievements and lessons learned in leadership. Keller is the founder of the largest real estate agency in the United States, Keller Williams Realty. He is also a best-selling author and a successful business coach. Over the years, he's learned to achieve success in a rather unconventional way.

Keller intentionally started focusing on fewer things so he could focus on the *ONE Thing* that created momentum for everything else to happen. You want completing your one priority thing to have a domino effect on future tasks and initiatives. Therefore, you want to take the smallest action right now so that connected future actions that currently seem daunting are either easier or perhaps even unnecessary.

A well-documented relationship exists between parent involvement and student performance (Mapp & Kuttner, 2013). In an effort to increase parental involvement and engagement at the Male Leadership Academy in Charlotte, North Carolina, the instructional team set a goal to increase home-school communication. We started out with simple home-school communication improvements, such as increasing timely response to teacher emails and phone calls by parents (more on this strategy in chapter 7). As the school leader, the first small thing I did was take a few minutes to research how many parents were using our school's parent portal. I found that only 20 percent of parents used the portal consistently and effectively. Therefore, very little communication and connection between parents and teachers took place around academics, and by the time it did, teachers were often delivering bad news.

I decided to do one thing to get the ball rolling. One thing that would spark an improvement in home-school communication around academics before it was too late. I decided to make sure the sign-up process for the portal was parent friendly. I set up computers at the next parent-teacher conference and personally walked all parents through how to sign up and access the parent portal. Additionally, I created a parent-friendly video of me walking a parent step-by-step through the sign-up process.

This one small step of making the sign-up process parent friendly empowered parents to use the portal and get real-time access to attendance, behavior, and academic information, which changed the way teachers and parents engaged about academics. Over one semester, the number of parents enrolled and active in the parent portal increased from 20 percent to 60 percent. This new communication allowed us to build valuable rapport with families and students, which we needed later to knock down larger performance and behavior dominos.

Staying Focused by Asking a Question

To stay focused on our priorities—our one thing—throughout the day, we need to get good at asking the same question individually and institutionally. Why a question instead of a statement? Well, questions direct our focus, and engage our critical thinking. When we ask a question, our brain will always try to answer it. Asking better questions allows us to get to the root cause and our brains to come up with better answers (Serrat, 2017). But what question should we ask?

To find the question at the heart of your moment-by-moment effectiveness in school, we might again turn to Keller. He regularly asked himself a guiding question: "What's the ONE Thing I can do, such that by doing it, everything else will be easier or unnecessary?" (Keller & Papasan, 2013, p. 106).

Of course, real estate is different from education. As I considered whether this focus question would work for educators, I realized that unlike in the business world, in education we must understand that few things exist regarding content or standards that we have the power to make unnecessary. However, we do have the power to make learning easier. We can also make some disruptive behaviors and their corresponding punishments unnecessary. Therefore, I call the following the *educator's focus question*: What's the one thing I can do for my students, such that by doing it, everything else I do with my students becomes easier or unnecessary? Asking ourselves this question gives us personal peace of mind, so the task before us doesn't overwhelm us. Institutionally, it refocuses everyone in the building on the most important thing every day in every situation. Always remember that you can't complete the large task until the smallest task is completed first.

POWERIDEA

What's the one thing I can do for my students, such that by doing it, everything else I do with my students becomes easier or unnecessary?

This question shapes our thinking in the following ways.

- It reminds us that there is no free lunch in parenting our children or teaching students. If we want something from students, we must give something to them. It is selfish for us to think otherwise.

- It reminds us that we cannot have multiple simultaneous priorities if we are to be peak performers. Therefore, only one priority exists, or one most important thing that will assist you in achieving all other priorities.

- It shifts your focus to the powerful impact that small daily actions have on future conflicts, challenges, and successes.

- It helps one thing to rise to the surface and causes everything else to fade away.

- It acts as a stress reducer to refocus us on the one thing that changes everything.

Next, we will look for the answer to the educator's focus question.

Discovering the One Thing: Relationships

Relationships are the answer to the educator's focus question. The evidence for this is within a groundbreaking report by the Achievement Gap Initiative (AGI) at Harvard University (Ferguson, 2015). Researchers administered 300,000 surveys in more than 16,000 classrooms, 490 schools, twenty-six districts, and fourteen states. The team analyzed the surveys and created the Seven Cs of Effective Teaching (Ferguson, 2015).

1. **Care:** Show concern for students' emotional and academic well-being.

2. **Confer:** Encourage and value students' ideas and views.

3. **Captivate:** Spark and maintain student interest in learning.

4. **Challenge:** Insist that students persevere and do their best work.

5. **Classroom management:** Foster orderly and on-task classroom behavior.

6. **Clarify:** Help students understand content and resolve confusion.

7. **Consolidate:** Help students integrate and synthesize key ideas.

Notice that the first five of the Seven Cs of Effective Teaching as listed here have nothing directly to do with reading, writing, and arithmetic but everything to do with relationships. They let your students know that you are sincerely interested and invested in who they are as people. The first five Cs let your students know that you are invested and interested in what happened to them yesterday and last night that may affect them today. The first five Cs also convey that you are interested and invested in anything today that may affect their tomorrow. Finally, the first five Cs tell your students that you care about their tomorrow and that's why you push them to be their best today.

At this point, the final two Cs (clarify and consolidate) are made infinitely easier when it is clear to the student that you are interested and invested holistically in them as people and not just their performance on paper. For this reason, beginning with chapter 3, each power move or strategy is proven to be the catalyst for building healthy relationships with students and their families. Frankly, the relationship between teacher and student is the straw that stirs the classroom and school culture drink. While students are in school, it is this relationship that fuels academic engagement and inspires lifelong learning. The Seven Cs help to confirm that the one thing we need to prioritize with students is healthy relationships.

Needing Caring Human Relationships

In almost every classroom around the globe, high standardized test scores are the goal of students, the measure of teacher productivity, and almost the primary focus of teacher accountability. Reading, writing, and arithmetic are important, but we often miss a key component to helping teachers and students accomplish their mutual goal of high performance: Supportive teacher-student relationships are a critical factor in creating and maintaining a sense of school belonging that encourages positive academic and behavioral outcomes. These positive outcomes shape classroom and school culture (Mason, Hajovsky, McCune, & Turek, 2017). See figure 1.1 (page 14).

However, partially and fully disengaged students often have poor attendance records, rarely participate in class or school activities, don't become cognitively involved in learning or fully develop persistence, nor do they self-regulate their behavior toward goals. Without a healthy intervention, disengaged students will most likely go on to become partially or fully disengaged citizens.

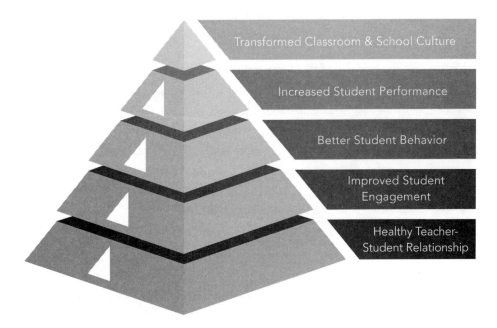

Figure 1.1: Healthy teacher-student relationships lead to a healthy school culture.

Don't just take it from me. One of my former students, Calesia House, is director of instrumental music at the school where she teaches. The following is what she says about the power of relationships:

> My family had a hard time trusting institutions because of their firsthand experience with institutions failing them. The institutions failed us, not just black people, people of color, but poor people. My grandmother was born in 1921 and lived through the Great Depression. She only received a fourth-grade education because there were "not enough colored teachers to teach the colored children." My mother was born in 1961, and she went to a segregated school until she was eleven! This was not that long ago. Many of my team members are the same age as my mother.
>
> We (black people and poor people) do not have a great relationship with institutions—schools, banks, government, and so on. So, if and when the school systems or teachers reach out, we are immediately hesitant because of the generational history with these institutions. The only way to break these barriers is to develop meaningful and true relationships with your students and their families of all backgrounds and socioeconomic situations; have

grace, have compassion. Once you can develop a relationship with the child, hopefully, the child will start to erase the generational curse. (C. House, personal communication, January 7, 2021)

Jessica Tavares, Newark Board of Education's 2022 Teacher of the Year, makes sure that she models acceptance and kindness in her classroom, saying "When you actually want to be in school and feel like you are accepted, you are more willing to try your best" (as cited in Carrera, 2022).

The best educators have long understood the importance and power of connecting with and valuing other human beings. One example of the power of relationships is the still-face experiment by M. Katherine Weinberg and Edward Z. Tronick, developmental and clinical psychologists at Harvard University (Weinberg & Tronick, 1996). The still-face experiment shows that babies are extremely responsive to emotions and their social interactions with the world around them, and that the absence of that feedback is harmful to development and healthy attachment.

For example, in the first phase of the still-face experiment, a parent sits down and plays with her baby (Weinberg & Tronick, 1996). The baby starts pointing at different places in her world, and the mother engages and plays with her. The mother works to coordinate her emotions and her intentions with her baby, which is what the baby usually experiences. Then the psychologist asks the mother to stop engaging with the baby and just look at the baby with a still face. The baby quickly picks up on this total disengagement and uses all her abilities to try to engage the mother. First, she smiles at the mother. Next, she points. Third, the baby puts both hands up in front of the mother as if to say, "What's happening here?" Finally, she screeches at the mother as if to say, "Come on, why are we doing this?" The baby reacts negatively as quickly as two minutes after not receiving normal engagement. The baby turns away and seems to experience stress from the parental disengagement. The baby loses control and frantically reaches for her mother. The study reinforces that we need human interaction to function in the world fully (Weinberg & Tronick, 1996).

In 2020, the COVID-19 pandemic affected the world. Italy instituted a mandatory lockdown for its sixty million citizens (Mahbubani & Ma, 2020). In the United States, K–12 schools and universities suspended in-person learning for at least two weeks, and some closed for the rest of the school year. Around the globe, schools moved most of their instruction online. Online platforms and video services such as Skype and Zoom substituted for in-person classrooms, and engagement through technology replaced human engagement. According to a 2019 report, "Online students desire greater student-instructor interaction, and the online education community is also calling for a stronger focus on such interactivity to address a widely recognized shortcoming of current online offer-ings" (Protopsaltis & Baum, 2019, p. 2).

Since "online education is the fastest-growing segment of higher education, and its growth is overrepresented in the for-profit sector" (Protopsaltis & Baum, 2019, p. 2), some might argue that nothing is missing when a student receives 100 percent online instruction. Unfortunately, that is a false assertion. What's missing is the ability to form healthy human relationships. What's missing is the opportunity for chemistry to occur between students and their teachers and peers. What's missing is the feedback loop between teacher and student during teacher-guided practice. What's missing is the ONE Thing that changes everything: healthy, caring relationships. Each of the seven power moves starting in chapter 3 (page 31) points to these ingredients as their foundation.

Knowing Your Effect Size

It's fair to wonder, when thinking about teacher-student relationships, how much of our understanding of their importance is informed by more than subjective observation and interpretation. It's fair to ask, how does a lack of teacher-student relationship affect students, academically or behaviorally? Since educators have limited time and resources, and so much to do, one key thing they need to know is the effect or impact certain strategies have on students. A good way to know your effect on students is to understand the effect size of your actions. The *effect size* is the demonstrated degree of impact you have on learning.

John Hattie's (2009) book *Visible Learning: A Synthesis of Over 800 Meta-Analyses Relating to Achievement* combined thousands of individual studies involving mil-lions of students worldwide to find what was working in education. According to Hattie, *visible learning* occurs when teachers see learning through the eyes of stu-dents and help them become their own teachers. He lists and ranks 195 factors that impact student achievement and their effect sizes. The strength or impact of the effect measures from –0.51 to 1.57 (Hattie, 2009). In 2017, Hattie updated his list of factors from 195 to 256 (Visible Learning, 2017). Teacher-student relationships is still on that list, and I would argue they impact all other factors.

Positive effect sizes from 0.10 to 0.20 indicate an action that does not improve student learning, when looking at the learning impact over the course of a full school year versus not having taken that action. Effect sizes of 0.30 to 0.40 are considered moderate, indicating actions a teacher might take in their classroom. Anything over 0.40 is considered a strong effect. If you average everything we do in education, the effect size is about 0.40; thus, Hattie calls this the hinge point or the benchmark where learning turns (Hattie, 2009).

The goal is to strive for strategies that impact your students at least 0.40 and upward. For instance, no strategy under 0.40—even though it might show improvement—has enough impact or effect for one year's growth over a school year. In other words, strategies under 0.40 do not have the fuel needed to move the learning needle. Anything at or above 0.50 is excellent because it has an effect size beyond one year of growth.

Hattie's updated research in 2017 has *collective teacher efficacy*, which is the collective belief of teachers in their ability to positively affect students, as one of the top two actions with the greatest effect sizes (Donohoo, Hattie, & Eells, 2018). Which includes students who are disengaged and disadvantaged. Collective teacher efficacy has an effect size of 1.57! That represents the collective belief that our students can learn.

However, as we review Hattie's 256 factors related to achievement, the input and influence of the teacher emerge with an effect size of 0.72. More importantly, it is the only one of his 256 strategies that have mutual and multiple benefits for both teachers and students. Collective teacher efficacy is at the top of Hattie's list because teachers and students are in a mutually beneficial positive feedback loop.

Feedback loops are created when reactions affect themselves and create a positive or negative cause-and-effect loop. For example, consider the cruise control that regulates a car's speed. If you set the cruise at 55 mph and drive downhill, the car responds by decreasing the speed based on the desired setting of 55 mph, which is an example of cause and effect. As researcher Binu Pathippallil Mathew puts it, "Positive feedback has the power to initiate further action and it improves both teaching and learning. Feedback and instruction are intertwined" (Binu, 2020). However, educators must recognize the difference between feedback and praise. Praise tells a student, "Good job!" Feedback tells the student why they were successful (Hattie & Yates, 2014).

When teachers believe in students and create sincere, performance-based relationships, their reward is active and enthusiastic students who do more than attend or perform academically. Students also put forth effort, persist, self-regulate their behavior toward goals, challenge themselves to excel, and enjoy challenges and learning (Christenson, Reschly, & Wylie, 2012).

When students respond positively to this caring teacher-student relationship, their feedback inspires teachers' efforts, increases job satisfaction, and decreases job stress. Not only is a positive feedback loop created, but with healthy teacher-student engagement, there is one other unique benefit. This benefit is not strictly academic, and it may be even more beneficial to students than learning to read. Healthy teacher-student engagement provides students with a better vision of their lives. One could say it provides students with hope!

Finally, if you take healthy teacher-student relationships away, all 256 strategies fall apart. So, for any strategy to have its true effect size, teachers and students must have healthy performance-based relationships. This context for relationships helps to answer our focus question: What's the one thing I can do for my students such that doing so makes everything else I do easier or unnecessary?

The one thing all educators can do is develop sincere, positive relationships with students that foster effective learning. When that happens, everything changes! Performance-based relationships are the one thing that changes everything because they are the first domino that starts the chain reaction and knocks down all the other learning dominos! Please see figure 1.2 for an illustration of this concept.

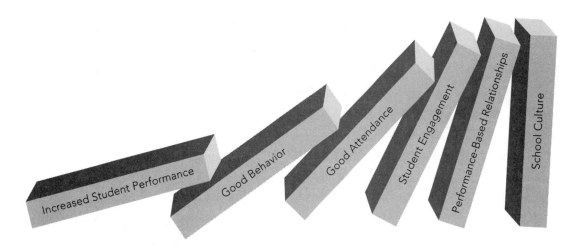

Figure 1.2: The domino effect of performance-based relationships.

Many educators believe the first domino is out of their control and that other dominos must fall before increased student performance is possible. For instance, some believe students should arrive at school and enter their classroom with eagerness and excitement for learning. In their defense, that belief is often true, and that domino has fallen for the engaged students who arrive each day focused and ready to learn. However, partially engaged and disengaged students have a better chance of improving their academic performance once the performance-based relationships domino has been established and has fallen.

My Big Three Chapter Reflections

The following questions can help you reflect on the concepts discussed in chapter 1.

1. If improving parental engagement is the big domino that you want to knock down, what are the smaller dominos that would ultimately knock down your big domino?

2. List a major initiative in your classroom or school. How might relationships with students and their families affect the outcomes of the program? What are the smaller dominos that would ultimately knock down your big domino?

3. Write the names of two students from your *partially engaged* or *disengaged* groups you want to build a better performance-based relationship with. How might you begin to do this?

CHAPTER 2

Get Our Buts Out of the Way:
Relationship Mindsets

Whether you think they can or they can't, you're right.

—Baruti K. Kafele

The following story helps explain the power of relationships and their effect on student engagement. One early cold morning in Michigan, my wife and I prepared to run errands. I had an older car, so I went outside to warm it up. The car would not start, but lights came on, and the stereo worked. I called AAA automobile service to report a dead battery. When the AAA representative arrived, he informed me that the battery was not dead. If it was, nothing would operate. However, some vehicle accessories will operate if the battery has a low voltage because some functions only require a small amount. But, if you want the engine to start and move the car forward, the automobile battery must have a higher voltage.

In schools, student and family engagement are the engine, and performance-based relationships are the battery. With low-level teacher-student relationships, lower-level functions will continue to operate; however, if we want high-level engagement and high-level performance, it's best to have a higher-level teacher-student relationship. I can't emphasize enough that high-level teacher-student relationships are suitable for all students but are particularly important for partially engaged and disengaged students (Beattie, Rich, & Evans, 2015). With all the evidence we have today regarding the transformational benefits of engagement, you have to wonder what's stopping us from going all-in with strategies that prioritize building healthy performance-based teacher-student relationships with *all* students.

In this chapter, you will learn about the three educator mindsets: (1) culture-driven mindset, (2) competence-driven mindset, and (3) coach-driven mindset. Then we explore each mindset and in what situations they are most effective. This discussion will set you up for the first power move discussed in chapter 3 (page 31), which is to adopt the classroom coach mindset.

In *Professional Learning Communities at Work: Best Practices for Enhancing Student Achievement*, educator Richard DuFour describes schools that operate under quite different assumptions—these schools believe all students can learn at high levels, but they respond to students who are not learning in significantly different ways (DuFour & Eaker, 1998).

For several years, I worked with public and private districts performing school culture and student engagement audits. While conducting the observations, I could see that all the schools believed that all students could learn. However, administrators and teachers built relationships with students differently based on their own mindsets, which heavily influenced student and family engagement. Educators who held two of the three mindsets (the culture and competence mindsets) built relationships with all students but deeper ones with students who were more aligned with their own mindsets. During the audit, I observed that the culture and competence mindsets were formed from personal experiences that shaped personal biases, which drove teacher-student relationships and engagement. However, educators who held the third mindset (the coach mindset) built performance-based relationships with *all* students and did everything short of mandating resources and input from all other stakeholders! Table 2.1 outlines these three mindsets and how they impact teacher-student relationships and student engagement.

These three relationship mindsets directly affect academic and behavior performance because they drive student engagement, teaching strategies, and policies on how students are supported or punished. Ultimately, these three mindsets help to shape the classroom and overall school culture.

POWERIDEA

Their personal *buts* prevented them from building healthy, inspiring, performance-based relationships with *all* students and *all* families.

To be clear, my school audits and observations overwhelmingly found that all teachers build relationships! However, their personal *buts* prevented them from building healthy, inspiring, performance-based relationships with *all* students and *all* families. These buts represent several relationship mindsets and hurdles, which directly affect student engagement, behavior, and performance, and ultimately shape school culture.

Table 2.1: The Three Educator Mindsets

Mindset	Description	Who Benefits
Culture-driven mindset	These educators build relationships with all students, *but* they build deeper performance-based relationships with students who comply or connect with their personal or classroom culture.	Partially engaged and disengaged students and their families who most likely represent the cultural viewpoints or representations of their teacher.
Competence-driven mindset	These educators build relationships with all students, *but* they build deeper performance-based relationships with students who they believe have the cognitive ability to succeed in their class.	Engaged students because they prove the theory of this particular fixed mindset.
Coach-driven mindset	These educators use compassionate accountability and the resources of stakeholders to build performance-based relationships with all students and their families, regardless of culture, condition, or competency.	Engaged, partially engaged, and disengaged students and their families because they each receive acceptance for their unique needs, viewpoints, or representations from their teacher.

In *Transforming School Culture*, educator Anthony Muhammad (2018) writes that a positive school culture is a place where:

> Educators have an unwavering belief in the ability of all their students to achieve success, and they pass that belief on to others in overt and covert ways. Educators create policies and procedures and adopt practices that support their belief in every student's ability. (p. 20)

Culture is the entirety of how we do things and what we believe. How we do things is frequently created by what Muhammad (2018) calls *perceptual predetermination*: "An educator's own socialization and the impact of that socialization on his or her practice in the classroom, including expectations for student performance" (p. 31). This perceptual predetermination drives a teacher's approach to building relationships with students. That's why it's crucial to address our buts and get them out of the way.

This chapter explores the culture-driven, competence-driven, and coach-driven mindsets and their effects on the classroom. We then wrap up with some chapter reflections.

The Culture-Driven Mindset

Educators who hold a culture-driven mindset build relationships with all students, *but* they build deeper performance-based relationships with students who comply or connect with their personal or classroom culture. Take a moment to think about three different dining experiences: one at a high-end fine dining restaurant, and the other two at one of your favorite fast-food restaurants. For me, I would think about Ruth's Chris Steak House for my fine dining experience. For fast-food, I would think about McDonald's and Chick-fil-A.

All three places certainly engage me, but each one engages me differently based on their dining expectations for their customers and my behavior in their restaurant. Their dining expectations are shaped by processes, procedures, and people that inform each restaurant's cultural mindset. My behavior combined with their mindset drives my experience and level of engagement in each restaurant.

I'm often asked, "Shouldn't students comply with or obey those who are in authority or responsible for them?" My response is, "Yes!" However, the *but* in this mindset is not about teachers' concern that their authority is being undermined. Instead, this mindset is rooted in a teacher's cultural comfort and connection level with the student.

In culture-driven classrooms, students who best meet the teacher's institutional, cultural, academic, or behavioral expectations receive higher teacher feedback and praise than those who don't. Teacher educator Zaretta Hammond said during her interview with Edthena (2023) that "All instruction is culturally responsive; the question is to whose culture is it responding?" Table 2.2 describes some cultural connections.

Table 2.2: Cultural Connections

Cultural Connections	Descriptions
Ethnicity and language	Student shares the teacher's ethnicity and language.
Geographic connection	Student shares the teacher's local or international home origins.
Sports	Student shares the teacher's athletic experiences or philosophies.
Gender	Student shares the teacher's gender philosophies.
Politics	Student shares the teacher's political philosophies.
Religion	Student shares the teacher's faith.
Classroom rules	Student is behaviorally compliant.

If a student looks and acts in the culturally expected or respected ways, they get more of the teacher's positive attention. *But* if a student does not, the teacher-student relationship is consciously or unconsciously minimized.

Educators with a culture-driven mindset can verbally assert and show that they believe in every student's ability; however, their but gets in the way of building a healthy performance-based relationship that drives engagement. In this case, the level of the relationship with students is driven by the student's ability or willingness to comply with cultural norms such as language, dialect, dress, and even hairstyle. While educators with a culture-driven mindset will interact with all students, their but short-circuits the willingness to provide enough relationship voltage to turn on motivation and learning for *all* students.

The Competence-Driven Mindset

Educators who hold a competence-driven mindset build relationships with all students, *but* they build deeper performance-based relationships with students who they believe have the cognitive ability to succeed in their class. Educators with this mindset believe a student's ability to learn has already been fixed by nature or nurture. Therefore, a meaningful teacher-student relationship is targeted to those students who are believed to possess the intelligence needed to perform the work. For those who don't fit into this category, the teacher-student relationship is reduced from high-level expectation to mere interaction.

The competence-driven mindset does not readily accept the malleability of intelligence. Instead, this mindset believes that a student has been given a specific amount of intelligence, and it cannot be altered, or at least it is highly stable across time. In her seminal work *Mindset: The New Psychology of Success*, Carol Dweck (2016) popularly coined this position as the *fixed mindset*.

It could also be said that the competence-driven mindset is a disciple of the controversial book *The Bell Curve: Intelligence and Class Structure in American Life* (Herrnstein & Murray, 1994). In their book, psychologist Richard Herrnstein and political scientist Charles Murray (1994) argue that the gaps between the groups we see in society are not socially created but are manifestations of differences in cognitive ability as measured through the intelligent quotient (IQ) test.

Lurking behind such fixed mindsets is a simple question: If you're somebody when you're smart, what are you when you're not? As journalist Amy Waldman of *The New York Times* (1999) puts it, "Failure has been transformed from an action—failing at a business or other venture—to an identity."

The engaged students, particularly students in Advanced Placement classes, are served well with this mindset. However, this mindset has consequences for the teacher-student relationship and student achievement because it preselects or presorts students for victory. This unconscious bias can often be detected by students who are disengaged or not advanced, which causes them to put up a barrier between themselves and the teacher, further preventing a closer teacher-student relationship. This disengagement is now not about content but about connection. A personal connection that affects personal performance.

The Coach-Driven Mindset

Educators with a coach-driven mindset initiate and extend themselves to students. They use compassionate accountability and stakeholder resources to build performance-based relationships with all students and their families, regardless of culture, condition, or competency.

In chapter 3 (page 31), I unpack the profile and strategies of having a coach-driven mindset (the first power move). For now, it's essential to know that this mindset has no *but* because it sees students as individuals and the families as contributing team members. Therefore, all students are engaged with the expectation that they can and will contribute to their individual growth and the class's overall performance.

Unlike the fixed mindset that forms the basis of the competence-driven mindset, those with a coach-driven mindset believe intelligence (the ability to acquire knowledge and skills) is malleable and can be changed through effort and persistence. This growth mindset is associated with learning goals, mastery-oriented strategies, and beliefs in positive effort (Blackwell, Trzesniewski, & Dweck, 2007; Burnette, O'Boyle, VanEpps, Pollack, & Finkel, 2013). The coach mindset views trials as ways of succeeding toward desired outcomes and mastery. Teachers with this mindset believe that the brain and behavior are not fixed and can be changed, which is the coach's biggest weapon against ignorance and failure. Consequently, they pass their beliefs onto students who learn that they can develop their abilities and see barriers and teacher feedback as supports to help their learning.

While the coach's goal for the student is always content mastery, the student is also measured and motivated by their progress toward mastery. While students may have some idea about their academic performance relative to others in the class, what is valued and honored is their personal effort and progress toward mastery of course objectives.

Educators with a coach-driven mindset understand that there is a healthy tension and connection between the teacher's strength and the student's effort. Researcher Robert J. Marzano, whose Marzano Teacher Evaluation Model has been adopted by school districts in all fifty U.S. states to help teachers improve their instruction over time, believes that great teachers make great students (Marzano Center, 2017).

Educators with a coach-driven mindset engage all students and their families to ensure that everyone is involved and understands what they need to contribute to the team. Therefore, they are most likely to have enough engagement voltage to turn on motivation and learning in all students.

Ultimately, a big part of a student's success depends on having one or more teachers who genuinely believe they can learn and grow over time. Marzano's research has proven that the student who spends two years in a most effective school with a most effective teacher rockets to the ninety-sixth achievement percentile. According to Marzano, a most effective school where you are likely to find most effective teachers will have the following attributes (Marzano, 2012).

- A safe and orderly environment that supports cooperation and collaboration
- An instructional framework that develops and maintains effective instruction in every classroom
- A guaranteed and viable curriculum focused on enhancing student learning
- A standards-referenced system of reporting student progress
- A competency-based system that ensures student mastery of content

Remember, all students need is one or more effective teachers who believe in them. Are you the one? The converse also holds. If this same student spends two years in a least-effective school with a least-effective teacher, that student's achievement level plunges to the third percentile (Marzano, 2003).

Many of your partially engaged and disengaged students need you to have this mindset for them to improve their chance at success in life. If we genuinely want to revolutionize our school culture, we must get our engagement buts out of the way. So, what are your buts? Are there things you believe about your students that prevent you from giving them the rich and challenging classroom they need to thrive? How can you challenge those beliefs that keep you from being the teacher students need to help them truly succeed?

My Big Three Chapter Reflections

The following questions can help you reflect on the concepts discussed in chapter 1.

1. What is an example of possible effects of the coach-driven mindset on partially engaged students?

2. What is an example of possible effects of the competence-driven mindset on disengaged students?

3. What is an example of possible effects of the culture-driven mindset on partially engaged students?

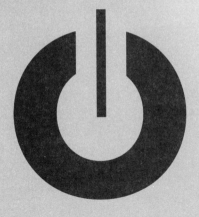

PART 2

Implementation

CHAPTER 3

Power Move: Adopt the Classroom Coach Mindset

Without relationships, our students become points and percentages.

—Marcus Jackson

Growing up in Detroit, we frequently spent days at my grandmother's house. We didn't have very much, but my grandmother had a way of making magic happen in the kitchen. She went to the store and bought cheap, unseasoned, unprepared foods, took them into the kitchen, and turned them into a gourmet meal.

The mindset and skills to take what's given and enhance it separates the classroom coach mindset from all other mindsets. In contrast, other teachers may have the mindset and skill set best suited for enhancing already competent and culturally fit students. Just in case my mother reads this book, I must say I enjoyed my mother's cooking, but my grandmother had a different skill set and mindset with food than she did.

POWERIDEA

Mindset (n.d.) is "a fixed mental attitude or disposition that predetermines a person's responses to and interpretations of situations."

Mindsets are an important topic in social psychology. *Mindset* (n.d.) is "a fixed mental attitude or disposition that predetermines a person's responses to and interpretations of situations." The argument could be made that our mindset predetermines with whom and how we build relationships. It is why I encourage, if not beg, you to adopt the coach-driven mindset with your students.

During practice and games, a good coach fosters an athlete's belief that they can make mistakes but must try again. Then, a good coach offers direction and instruction and instills confidence that the athlete can keep improving. Finally, the good coach's belief in their athlete becomes the athlete's belief in themselves.

It is this mindset that a classroom coach takes into the classroom. A coach always believes that all their students can learn, improve, and contribute. They believe a mistake is just a mistake and not a permanent mark, lifetime ranking, or evaluation of who the person is. They always believe their student can achieve and, most importantly, make the student believe it, too.

I sometimes call this the *BAR code*. The *B* is for our *belief system*, which makes up our different mindsets in areas such as finance or faith. The *A* represents how our mindsets drive us to *act* as we set out to achieve or perform. And finally, the *R* stands for how we *respond* to certain situations based on our mindsets. What we believe directly informs how we act and respond. As teachers, we must recognize our mindsets or BAR code and how it affects our students. That's why power move number one must be about adopting a coach's mindset!

Do you want to be known primarily as a classroom teacher who has mastery over facts? Or do you want to be known as a classroom coach who can build relationships based on performance and inspire others to engage, learn, and master content? Certainly, the more successful teacher is not the one who knows the most about their subject. If that were the case, teacher interviews would simply be Praxis scores and a short pencil and paper test.

We know instead that the most successful teachers are the ones who help their students achieve. Teachers with a coach's mindset do not waste time trying to impress their students with their content knowledge; instead, they inspire them to learn. This chapter discusses the following four qualities that good classroom coaches possess.

1. Classroom coaches capture their students' hearts.

2. Classroom coaches believe in their students' competency.

3. Classroom coaches provide compassionate consequences.

4. Classroom coaches build a culture of community.

Before we dive into these four qualities, fill out the Classroom Coach's Creed in figure 3.1, and post it somewhere you'll see it every day to remind you of the valuable work you're doing.

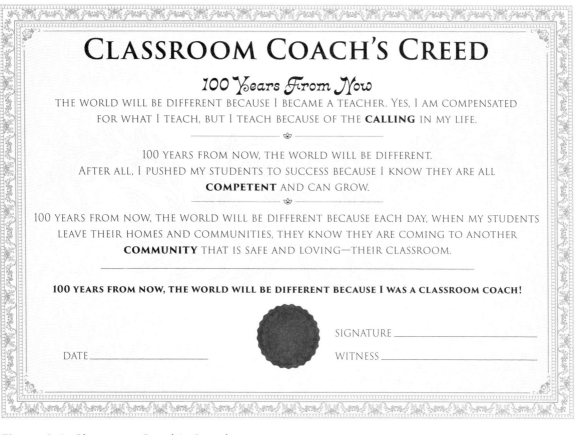

Figure 3.1: Classroom Coach's Creed.

*Visit **go.SolutionTree.com/studentengagement** for a free reproducible version of this figure.*

Classroom Coaches Capture Students' Hearts

Great coaches always try to win something or not lose something! In the classroom, this can translate to a healthy fear of losing students to the dangers of violence and poverty. They let this fear drive them. At the other end of this spectrum, the excitement of ensuring that students are prepared to win in the race of life also drives them. They want their students to win entrance to the best colleges or trade schools so they can become their best.

When you talk to classroom coaches or observe them teaching, you can hear it and see it, and their students feel it! Teaching is not something they *do*, teaching is who they are; it's what they *must* do. They have what I call a *south-to-north* teaching style. This teaching style first captures a student's heart and then moves north to the student's head. They deliver the curriculum wrapped in creativity and compassion. Students know that whatever happens in class, the teacher cares for them.

To understand why, let's look at Maslow's (1943) hierarchy of needs, which categorizes and prioritizes different needs from the bottom up (see figure 3.2). The bottom need is physiological (food, clothing, and so on), above that is safety, and above that is love and belonging (friendship). This level is the classroom coaches' secret sauce because they know it will be much easier to get students to the next levels (esteem and self-actualization) if the student feels close to the teacher. At the core, the primary mission of all seven power moves is capturing a student's heart. It's important not to look at the power moves simply as strategies to execute a lesson. While there are academic benefits to each power move, the goal is to help you capture your students' hearts, build relationships, and improve engagement.

Figure 3.2: Maslow's hierarchy of needs.

Because coaches aspire to meet students' love and belonging needs, they are most likely to have a positive teacher-student relationship quality (TSRQ). A TSRQ leads to more closeness than conflict between teachers and students. Researchers across multiple disciplines suggest that TSRQ has a strong association with positive student outcomes across all domains of student functioning (Poklar, 2018). One meta-analysis that included ninety-two peer-reviewed articles and over 129,000 students supported that TSRQ predicts achievement pathways, particularly for lower-achieving (disengaged) students and students in higher grades (Mason, Hajovsky, McCune, & Turek, 2017).

The best teachers understand how education fits in with the student's present situation and in the overall arc of the student's life. They can see not just this moment but years down the road when self-mastery will help their students keep a job, get a promotion, meet a goal, or raise students of their own.

To help improve student relationships, identify a student you struggle with more than others and who would benefit from having a greater relationship with you as their classroom coach. Then give them a filled-out Personal Act of Service or Sacrifice (PASS) form (see figure 3.3). The PASS is not for every student. It works best for disengaged students who, for whatever reason, you have not been able to connect with on a personal level. Perform a PASS that is unique for that student. (For example, supporting them at one of their sporting events or going out of your way to support their aspirations.) A key point to remember is that a PASS is not based on academic merit. It is based on your observation and desire to build a better relationship with a student by entering their world or sharing a part of yours. In addition, a PASS is not for every student and is given on an as-needed basis based on your capacity.

Personal Act of Service or Sacrifice (PASS)

Date: _____ Student Name: _____ Grade: _____

I will _____

_____

_____

Figure 3.3: Personal Act of Service or Sacrifice (PASS) form.

*Visit **go.SolutionTree.com/studentengagement** for a free reproducible version of this figure.*

Classroom Coaches Believe in Their Students' Competency

Teachers need to familiarize themselves with information about the school and state expectations, then investigate the composition of their classes and formulate a plan for classroom operation. Equipped with this information and a plan, teachers can then proceed to establish general academic expectations as well as individual student expectations.

What's not often talked about is that there are two parts to student expectations. The first part is the expectations set by the curriculum, district, and state. The second—and probably the most important—is each teacher's belief about their students and how they communicate those beliefs. Motivational speaker Zig Ziglar told a story about the famous archer Howard Hill, who won every archery contest in his life (as cited in Center for Performance Improvement, 2017). As the story goes, Howard Hill could split an arrow from fifty feet. Ziglar would go on to tell the crowd that he could teach them to shoot better than Howard Hill in twenty minutes, provided he first blindfolded Howard Hill.

As the audience roared with laughter, he shared the mighty lesson in his story that "The hardest target to hit is a target that you can't see" (as cited in Center for Performance Improvement, 2017). I often tell the same story using the Howard Hill example, but I share an additional, different ending. I say to superintendents, school leaders, and teachers everywhere that, yes, Mr. Ziglar is correct that the hardest target to hit is the one you can't see. But another very difficult target to hit is one you don't believe in for your students!

One study has shown that what we believe drives what we truly expect students to achieve.

> The pedagogical beliefs (for example, beliefs or 'mindsets' concerning the malleability of intelligence) that teachers hold may have a far-reaching impact on their teaching behavior. In general, two basic mindsets can be distinguished with regard to the malleability of intelligence: fixed (entity) and growth (incremental). (De Kraker-Pauw, Van Wesel, Krabbendam, & Van Atteveldt, 2017)

This finding highlights the impossibility of getting students to hit a target that you don't believe they can hit. Therefore, classroom coaches start the education process with the belief that all students can learn and learn at high levels. In fairness to teachers, one must remember that students have varied abilities. *High expectations* is a relative term since educators must individualize expectations to every class and student, cumulatively forming the framework for the class. After coaches have set expectations, they have the responsibility to positively reaffirm the expectations for all students.

With positive proclamations from coaches, this approach dares the students to explore and maximize their full potential. In the end, coaches spare no energy or effort to ensure that students take advantage of all opportunities that come their way. Sometimes, the strategy calls for coaches to help students develop talents that they would not personally desire to develop. For students who jump at the opportunity to speak and lead, coaches may intentionally provide them oppor- tunities to support others and learn humility and collaboration.

In setting high expectations and believing that students can achieve them, class- room coaches move their attention from students' socioeconomic background, level of parent involvement, or any other demographics directly or indirectly blamed for student failure to focus on individual and collective achievements. The expectations set by coaches mirror how the coaches perceive the students. The higher expectations coaches set, the greater potential they see. Consequently, the coach's growth mindset will be a major determinant of the extent to which a student or class (team) grows or improves.

Driven by a growth mindset, coaches encourage their teams (their classes) to put more effort in facing failure or discouragement, persevere amid challenges, and persist whenever tasks and assignments appear difficult. For students who may initially shy away from speaking and leadership opportunities, coaches can intentionally place them in those positions to give them opportunities to succeed or fail in a safe environment where acceptance and support is readily available. Teachers need the spirit of never giving up deeply instilled in their minds since they are entrusted with the responsibility of transferring the same perseverance to their students.

Like coaches, teachers have no choice but to embrace their mindset's impact on their teaching and consequently adopt the growth mentality. A teacher cannot draft better players or recruit smarter students. And why would they want to? A teach- er's goal is to take students as they are and move them as far forward as possible.

Classroom Coaches Provide Compassionate Consequences

In many classrooms, behavior is the elephant in the room that often derails the best intentions of a teacher's lesson plan. In the past, many classrooms used practices that amounted to zero tolerance, which is a behavioral intervention that caused more damage to the teacher-student relationship than it's worth. Basically, the zero-tolerance policy conveys to students that, in their classroom, it is con- sequence over connection.

Zero tolerance took off as a trend in school discipline during the late 1980s. Under this policy, schools issued severe and automatic punishments for even minor infractions. According to many research reports, such as *The Failure of Zero Tolerance*, zero tolerance doesn't work (Skiba, 2014).

In the United States, students missed out on eleven million instructional days in a single academic year due to zero tolerance (Losen & Whitaker, n.d.). The report also revealed that out-of-school suspensions have a disproportionate impact on the most vulnerable and powerless: students of color. Black students lost 103 days per 100 students enrolled, which is eighty-two more days than the twenty-one days their White peers lost due to out-of-school suspensions (Losen & Whitaker, n.d.).

The goal is not to go from zero tolerance to zero discipline. The goal is to structure discipline in a way that results in healthy productive behavior. Classroom coaches understand that the relationships they build with students impact those students' behavior and effort. Teacher-student relationships are tested when emotions escalate and student behavior is not positive—that's when compassionate consequences are important. It is in that moment that consequences must target the behavior but be compassionate enough that they do not target the person.

POWERIDEA

It is in that moment that consequences must target the behavior but be compassionate enough that they do not target the person.

Many teachers ask, "When student behavior is negative, and it's time for discipline, why would you consider compassion?" The answer depends on the end goal. If the end goal is to rid yourself of the student quickly and efficiently because of their negative behavior, then a zero-tolerance philosophy and policy in your classroom or school are all you need. However, if the goal is to create a positive school and classroom climate, then I would ask you to consider another strategy.

Compassionate consequences make it clear to the student and the rest of the team (the class) that the coach is correcting behavior and not punishing to inflict harm. In addition, compassionate consequences discard the idea of penalty and emphasize discipline through accountability. At the Male Leadership Academy, I trained my team to consider the following three items when they had to respond to behavior.

1. **Stubbornness is not strange:** I did not treat students as if they were aliens because there was conflict. I knew boys were going to test me, but I also knew I could pass their test by being fair and consistent with all my responses and consequences. I also knew or believed that my students wanted me to pass their test.

2. **Soft is hard:** When I responded to student misbehavior, I kept my voice and eyes soft. I needed my body language to express acceptance as well as disappointment.

3. **Sell the choices:** I wanted my students to understand that the unavoidable consequences were intended to shape the behavior that would make them not only great citizens in their classroom, but also great citizens in their home and community.

Once I established these three items, I could deliver the consequences. The key is having a healthy school discipline framework and relationship in place before you deliver consequences.

Instead of defaulting to a menu of punishments, look at the research that examines the association of school discipline practices with feelings of school connectedness. Students who attend schools with high suspension rates report lower levels of school connectedness, attendance, and after-school participation, and more sick days (Babey, Wolstein, Becker, & Scheitler, 2019). Simply using punishment to remove the behavior does not work to achieve the goal of educating the student. The evidence suggests that punitive disciplinary approaches often fail and are unnecessary (Wynne, 2013).

Classroom coaches understand the connection between compassionate consequences and creating a positive school climate for all students. Classroom coaches develop multiple ways of executing compassionate consequences without derailing classroom instruction or destroying the student's dignity or belief in themselves. Consequences that let everyone in the classroom know that the coaches are still in charge. Consequences that hold students accountable for their behavior but also convey that teachers still care and want the best for them. Students and families already know you have a hammer; compassionate consequences prove to them that you also have a heart.

Classroom Coaches Build a Culture of Community

A classroom coach is not simply an extension of the curriculum. They are a bridge between the student's community and the classroom community. When students leave their living community—the community of their parents where they play and pray—they arrive at their second community, a learning community.

Much like a good living community considers the unique physical and mental needs and concerns of its residents and does all it can to provide for them, a learning community does the same, which is made explicit with tangible outcomes. It looks like classroom processes that create healthy, academic-based relationships with families, lower behavioral referrals, improved grades, and increased graduation rates. In contrast, a bad classroom community is made evident by disconnected families, a rise in student failure rates, absenteeism, rampant disrespect, bullying, or staff resignation.

The correlation between the culture and performance of an organization is both strong and significant, hence the need to decide what you want your classroom community culture to be and then design it. In *Transforming School Culture*, Muhammad (2018) explains the desire that most in the United States share to build an egalitarian system of education where all students can learn. However, schools have crafted institutional barriers that predetermine which students have access to the best learning opportunities, which creates what Muhammad (2018) calls *institutional predetermination*.

In contrast, classroom coaches craft bridges instead of barriers. These bridges help students feel they have left their living community and arrived at their learning community. In building a culture of community, classroom coaches deliberately promote a philosophy of connectedness, and the classroom feeling is "When I win, we win; when I lose, *we* lose; so, let's win together!"

One way classroom coaches build their community is by incorporating symbols, rituals, and traditions unique to their specific class that build a sense of belonging and something unique. While serving as head of school, one way we created community at the beginning of the school year was for each class to participate in their own community circle. While in that circle, students took the following steps.

- Students chose a community name for their class.
- Students chose values for their community.
- Students created or adopted rules for community conversations.

If a student was absent that day, or when a new student joined the community, they were greeted, welcomed, and made aware of the community's values and rules that the students had created and adopted.

This process does not miraculously happen overnight; it happens in a demanding and supportive environment. The environment is demanding because the teacher and the students have clear and high expectations not only for grade-level mastery but also for areas of growth and effort. As we keep our academic expectations high, we can also let our students know that we support them with the little things we do, such as letting them know that we noticed a change in their mood, a new haircut, or style of clothing, and so on. It is essential to lend a listening ear to let students know that we are concerned about their family.

To help your students build a culture of community, gather your students for a meeting. Provide each student with an agreement form, as shown in figure 3.4, and begin a discussion regarding community values. Facilitate the meeting but ensure that students feel they have input and ownership.

Directions: Fill each box with your ideas and beliefs. Sign your name on the bottom.

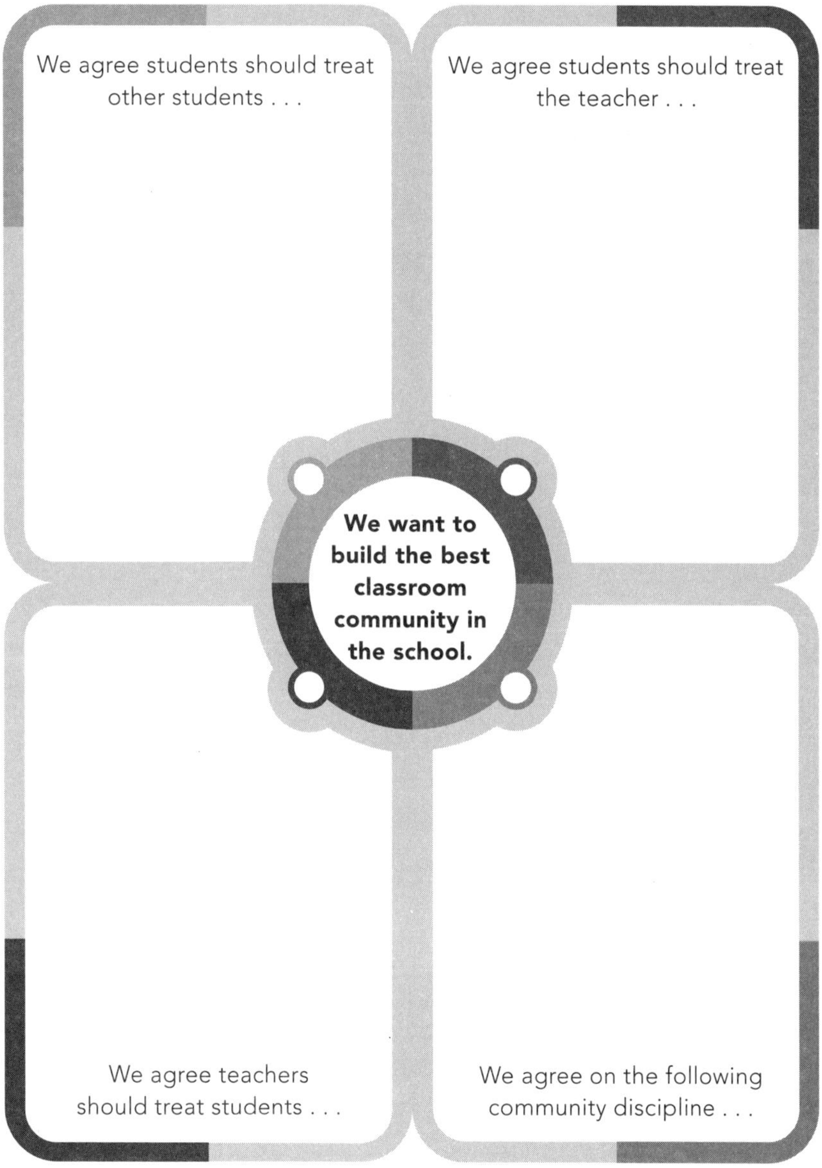

We agree students should treat other students . . .

We agree students should treat the teacher . . .

We want to build the best classroom community in the school.

We agree teachers should treat students . . .

We agree on the following community discipline . . .

Name _____ Date _____

Figure 3.4: Classroom community agreement.

*Visit **go.SolutionTree.com/studentengagement** for a free reproducible version of this figure.*

Now that we have discussed the power of the classroom coach mindset, it's time to turn our attention to helping you discover your *high why* for teaching.

CHAPTER 4

Power Move: Know Your *High Why* for Teaching

He who has a why to live for can bear with almost any how.
—Friedrich Nietzsche (as quoted by Victor Frankl)

Like other little boys, I got in trouble when I was young. Often, my parents asked, "Why did you do that?" My response was always, "I don't know." My dad always responded, "Well, if you don't know why you did it, then you had no purpose for doing it!" As a child I didn't know why he said that, but as an adult, I know that he was trying to teach me to think critically, make better decisions, and accept responsibility.

Many of my workshops for teachers start with a mindfulness exercise to get attendees thinking about their purpose or the *why* behind their decision to teach. The exercise is simple. I ask teachers to close their eyes and think back to when they chose their careers. Typically that's the time in their lives when they were most passionate and focused on the education profession. Teachers then share their passions for teaching and reasons they teach. After that, I share a few data points. I start by telling them that teaching is one of the most stressful occupations.

Around October, many teachers, especially young teachers, become emotionally and physically weakened and stressed. Everyone starts the school year rejuvenated from the summer and enthusiastic about what they plan to accomplish this year.

In October, the real world kicks in, with unexpected classroom behavior, unco-operative families, disagreements with colleagues or leadership, and the heavy workload. This high stress can cause teachers to burn out, disengage, and become dissatisfied with their jobs. It also increases turnover. According to a 2021 article published by the National Education Association, 32 percent of teachers say they plan to leave the profession entirely. That number was only 28 percent before the COVID-19 pandemic (Walker, 2021). During the pandemic, nearly half of the teachers who voluntarily left their positions during the school year offered COVID-19 as the reason (Diliberti, Schwartz, & Grant, 2021). However, the stress in teaching exists even outside of a pandemic.

Since the 1990s, researcher Richard Ingersoll at the University of Pennsylvania Graduate School of Education has studied the elementary and secondary teaching force. His updated longitudinal study on the transformation of the teaching force reports that 44 percent of new teachers leave teaching within five years (Ingersoll, Merrill, Stuckey & Collins, 2018). That attrition rate is even higher than the 40 percent of new police officers who leave within their first five years (Police Executive Research Forum, 2019).

As a past building leader, I'm very aware that education as a profession doesn't require training on how to deal with stress and trauma as part of the ongoing credentialing process. Most police, fire, and emergency management agencies require some amount of therapy after a traumatic incident. However, educators usually teach for thirty or more years with no mandatory process for addressing stress and trauma. This lack often causes them to hold many vicarious traumas from the students and families they serve.

This chapter explains the stress feedback loop and how your *high why*, or sense of purpose, connects to stress. Finally, we will discuss how to find your *high why*.

Stress Feedback Loop

When talking about stress, which both teachers and students bring to the classroom every single day, it's important to be clear that stress is normal. It's human to be stressed; it happens to everyone when you experience changes or challenges (stressors). In fact, our bodies are designed to experience stress and react to it (Cleveland Clinic, 2021). It is the body's reaction to a challenge or demand. But we also know that not all stress is good stress, and in the worst circumstances, it can become a toxic feedback loop between teachers and students.

According to the National Cancer Institute, "In medicine, stress is the body's response to physical, mental, or emotional pressure. Stress causes chemical changes in the body that can raise blood pressure, heart rate, and blood sugar levels" (Stress, n.d.). These changes can affect classroom teachers.

A report (Oberle & Schonert-Reichl, 2016) illustrates how stress becomes a contagion in the classroom when a teacher is stressed. Students can catch stress from burned-out teachers like they can the common cold. In essence, stressed teachers pass on stress to their students, who pass it back to their teachers. If they aren't careful, teachers and students can find themselves caught in a stress-feedback loop. For example, a stress-feedback loop can happen simply by having a very stressful conversation with a student's parent outside your classroom door and then returning to class to teach. Your level of enthusiasm is affected by the interaction, which infects your normal classroom delivery and engagement. Unfortunately, your lower level of engagement disengages your students, and their disengagement affects your delivery until you can recover from the encounter outside your classroom door.

POWERIDEA

A report (Oberle & Schonert-Reichl, 2016) illustrates how stress becomes a contagion in the classroom when a teacher is stressed. Students can catch stress from burned-out teachers like they can the common cold.

Therefore, when the teacher is stressed, the teacher-student relationship, which is the most powerful tool in the classroom, is working against everyone and limiting student engagement. Fortunately, as I explain in the next section, simply knowing your *high why* is a powerful means to disrupt this feedback loop.

Stress and Your *High Why*

The report showing stress as a classroom contagion specifically links classroom teacher burnout and cortisol levels in elementary school students (Oberle & Schonert-Reichl, 2016). *Cortisol* is the main stress hormone, which secretes into the bloodstream in large quantities in high-stress moments. Measuring it is a straightforward way to measure stress. Cortisol is best known for triggering the fight-or-flight instinct, and it works with certain parts of the brain to regulate mood, motivation, and fear.

But if stress is both good and bad, how do we differentiate? We have learned that there is a difference between *distress*, which uses cortisol for negative stress and *eustress*, which uses cortisol for positive stress (Li, Cao, & Li, 2016). One study identifies three levels within the cortisol profiles among children: (1) elevated, (2) moderate, and (3) low (Suor, Sturge-Apple, Davies, Cicchetti, & Manning, 2015). The study finds that students with relatively high or relatively low cortisol levels are more likely to experience learning deficits and cognitive delays. In addition, low levels of cortisol could be a biomarker for depression, apathy, or hopelessness. Elevated cortisol levels are linked to the distress caused by environmental stressors.

Why is this important? Moderate levels of cortisol also are linked to eustress, which means that the right amount of cortisol stimulates your passion and gives you the motivation needed to seize the day (Suor, Sturge-Apple, Davies, Cicchetti, & Manning, 2015). I call this moment where one has reached a moderate level of stress or eustress the *high why*, which is the sweet spot that exists when you are faced with a problem that causes stress, but your sense of purpose allows you to turn distress into eustress. This sweet spot is where you are cognitively aware of your teaching purpose and your why, but you are also at the next level—action and implementation. You have just enough stress to fuel your motivation to be creative, interactive, and more engaging.

Have you ever been there? Or have you ever seen one of your colleagues in their *high why* and wish you could be there with them? The first step is not to eliminate stress in the classroom but to find the happy medium between healthy stress and high expectations for teachers and students! The goal becomes to find your *high why* every day.

Road Back to *High Why*

Once you find that happy crossroad between high expectations and healthy stress, the joy of teaching can return. As BetterUp found in its research on work, "Building greater meaning in the workplace is no longer a 'nice-to-have' for companies, but a firm imperative for successful talent acquisition, retention, and growth" (Reece, Kellerman, & Robichaux, 2017).

If one has chosen to teach out of a vocational calling and not solely for compensation, it turns out that making money at work is much less valuable than having meaning at work. Meaning is the new money. That's why it's so important for you to know and to remember why you teach—knowing the why creates a sense of purpose and meaning mindset. The one who teaches with this mindset can instill a meaning for learning in their students.

For educators, the why often falls into one of several common categories. These are some of the responses I get when I ask teachers why they teach.

- "My teacher changed my life, and I want to return the favor."
- "I love to see a child's face when they finally understand a concept."
- "I love working with children more than adults."
- "It allows me to be with my children during their school breaks."
- "There's nothing more rewarding than transforming a life."

"Why teach?" is not a trivial question. Your why provides you with your intention and a far-reaching goal.

Having a strong sense of your why improves health and leads to greater fulfillment at work. For example, a growing body of findings from longitudinal epidemiological studies shows that a having a sense of purpose predicts reduced morbidity (for example, reduced risk of Alzheimer's disease, mild cognitive impairment, stroke, and myocardial infarction) and extended longevity (Kim, Kawachi, Chen, & Kubzansky, 2017). So, remembering why you chose to teach and teaching from that standpoint is not only good for your students, it also has a profound effect on the quality and quantity of your life!

Working with a purpose gives our lives more meaning. Meaning increases when we feel connected to others and something bigger than ourselves. Meaning helps us feel that we're an important part of a story with a beginning and end. It's not something only certain ethnic groups or genders possess. It's not even something that we must wait for a certain age to acquire. Meaning is about one's mindset. When someone's why exceeds GPAs and data points, they will behave in quite different ways. Think of the things one would do differently at work with meaning and purpose. Wouldn't meaning and purpose have an effect on attendance? Wouldn't meaning and purpose have an effect on relationships and conversations with colleagues? Of course they would!

In his book *HEART!*, educator Timothy D. Kanold (2017) provides a fine example of this mental space. He states that during a Solution Tree PLC Institute in 2016, he asked more than five hundred educators to define what passion in the workplace means. The following are the primary categories that describe the passion that he received from the prompt *Passion is . . .* :

> Passion is what I feel.
>
> Passion is what I love, and I love to teach.
>
> Passion is to be fully energized in my work.
>
> Passion is the emotion I bring to work every day.
>
> Passion is what helps me inspire my students.
>
> Passion is what serves me when I get tired.
>
> Passion is what sustains me in the moments of doubt.
>
> Passion is my burning desire to help difficult children.
>
> Passion is what motivates me to right the wrongs I see in my school.
>
> Passion is just my style. (Kanold, 2017, p. 14)

Dare I say that on that day, Kanold was in the presence of a group of *high why* educators! These educators possess a why and can take on the stress of the classroom. More than likely, they work in that rare space of eustress rather than distress.

Teachers who don't have a why can easily feel their work lacks meaning and are more likely to leave the classroom or feel dissatisfied with their students, families, and leadership. Most importantly, they are less likely to build healthy relationships with students and increase engagement.

Now, imagine a building filled with classroom coaches with *high why*. Imagine the types of relationships built with all students. Imagine the relationships built with families. Imagine how much joy you can have simply by remembering why you teach and teaching with purpose. The following sections offer some guidance to help you with this.

Consult With Your Inner Circle

Most of us have some kind of inner circle of people we trust. Maybe it's friends or family, maybe it's teacher colleagues or other people we interact with in our communities. These are valuable resources to lean on because they can help us on our journey. To help take advantage of this resource, use the reproducible "Know Your *High Why* for Teaching" to share your *high why* with your inner circle.

Create a High Why Journal

A journal can be invaluable to help keep us on track with our goals. Creating a journal can help you remember your purpose and avoid anything that will defeat that purpose. As you complete this power move, journey back to the time you made the choice to enter the field of education. Take a second to remember the excitement, purpose, and wisdom of your choice. While you are in that space, think about any person, place, or thing that could derail your opportunity to fulfill your purpose. Use the reproducible "My *High Why* Journal" (page 50) to explore your high why.

Now that we have explored your *high why*, we will explore helping your students find their *high why*.

Know Your *High Why* for Teaching

Directions: Remember that your *high why* is the purpose that is so important to you that it is greater than the problems you face fulfilling that purpose. Fill out this reproducible and share your *high why* for educating students with your inner circle of friends or family members. They can remind you of your teaching purpose in those moments when teaching becomes difficult.

It is thirty years from now, and you have retired. You have worked hard at being a great teacher. Write about your accomplishments.

Twenty years from now, you are at a restaurant, and a large group of your former students enter and sit behind you. They don't recognize you, and they start reminiscing about being in your class. What do they say about you and the effect your teaching had on their lives?

If you mentored new teachers, what personal advice and examples would you give them so that they could maintain their effectiveness and passion for teaching?

My *High Why* Journal

Directions: Your *high why* is the purpose that matters to you so much that it is greater than the problems you face fulfilling that purpose. Use this *high why* journal to plan how you will respond to your stress each week.

Month:_____

My *High Why* Week	This week I will commit to doing this to remind myself of my purpose for teaching.	This week I will commit to avoiding this, so I will not defeat my purpose for teaching.
Week One		
Week Two		
Week Three		
Week Four		
Special Observations		

CHAPTER 5

Power Move:
Help Students Find
Their *High Why*

If the purpose for learning is to score well on a test, we've lost sight of
the real reason for learning.

—Jeannie Fulbright

One September morning, my curriculum director knocked on my door. She wanted to discuss planning our next career day. At that time, I had hosted or spoken at more than two dozen career days at my school and elsewhere. I was a little bored with the traditional model of inviting professionals to talk to our students about their exciting careers. After brainstorming with my director, we came up with something that would change our career day forever. It also ended up being one of our largest school and Parent-Teacher Association (PTA) fundraisers.

We created the Male Leadership Academy's first student career museum. The following steps changed the game for us.

- Students decided which career they were interested in and visited www. bls.gov (U.S. Bureau of Labor Statistics) to research the career.

- Students wrote a short paper on their career's income, education needed, and future hiring projections.

- We invited our board members, parents, friends, vendors, and the community in collaboration with our school's PTA to purchase $1 raffle tickets to our students' career museum.

On museum day, students dressed up in their chosen career attire with props and took their stations in our gym. Visitors dropped one raffle ticket into a student's bucket, and the students acted out or read their career information to each visitor. Of course, visitors didn't just buy one raffle ticket; they bought $5 worth of tickets only to find out that they wanted to hear more. They came back and bought $10, $15, sometimes $20 worth of raffle tickets.

The students loved dressing up and acting out their careers. The parents loved to see their children and other students dress up and give them a view of what the future would look like. The teachers had a blast with this project-based learning opportunity. The school raised hundreds of dollars in collaboration with our PTA. And our students got to see how school directly connects with their chosen professions. Even our athletes saw firsthand how important English language arts and mathematics are to their dream of becoming a professional athlete. It was a win, win, win for everyone! It's a huge win for students to have a purpose because in those moments, days, and months when classwork seems tedious, they have a reason that is above the state's, their family's, and your mandates to learn. They gain their very own personalized and internalized reason for engaging.

This chapter discusses why students need a why, how not all whys are equal, and what to do when students don't know their why.

Why *High Why* Is Important to Your Students

After reflecting on the importance of chapter 4's exploration of knowing your *high why* as a teacher, consider this mindset in light of your students. How much more motivated or engaged do you think a student would be if they found their *high why* for learning? I can't imagine getting up early every day, getting dressed, and going to work without knowing my *high why*. So, every time I see students board a bus to school, I can't help but wonder if they have a reason or purpose for going to school. Do they have a *high why* for learning?

Since the early 2000s, I've had the pleasure of talking to and training thousands of parents. What is clear about the parents of engaged students is they take the time to ensure their children understand their family's why for learning. These forward-thinking families go a step further by helping their children identify their own specific *high why*, which is the purpose that matters so much that it is greater than the problems you face fulfilling that purpose. This *high why* also helps them build personal agency. Therefore, a *high why* is essential.

Agency can be defined as a student's ability, desire, and power to determine their own course of action (Vaughn, 2018). It is the opposite of helplessness. As students build agency, they begin to take more ownership of their own learning because they determine this learning benefits them personally. Don't we all want our students to take some level of ownership in their own learning?

Once students reach high school, their why becomes vital because a student's desired career path informs their choice of subjects. A student who has a *high why* to study medicine will certainly know which subjects to choose and what amount of engagement with the classes will yield the acceptable performance to secure admission to their desired school. Students attuned to the demands of their preferred career and professional journey do not study in a vacuum. They study and behave with clearly set short- and long-term objectives, guided by specific individual targets.

Students who know why they are learning are better at self-governing and choosing partners, behaviors, and places that support their *high why*. A student who knows and believes that their teacher is a part of the team that will help them accomplish their *high why* will build a better relationship with that teacher and be more engaged in class. To help you begin the conversation and journey to helping students connect their classes to their *high why*, use the reproducible "What Type of Person Do You Want to Be?" on page 53. Your students' answers can provide insight on topics to weave into your lessons.

Why All Whys Are Not Created Equal

While it is important that students have a why, it may be just as important to understand that there are different whys that drive them. Some whys begin from a desire to fix a problem, support family pride, avoid punishment, achieve material success, or achieve personal success (my favorite). I define *personal success* as something that you have enough passion to develop skill for and that generates legal income.

While all whys bring benefits, some have greater benefits than others. A longitudinal study of two thousand students by researchers David S. Yeager and colleagues (2014) documents a correlation between self-transcendent purpose for learning and academic self-regulation. In other words, exceeding one's own purpose for learning while regulating one's behavior to achieve their academic goals. Picture your classroom where your students are regulating their own behavior in an effort to achieve or exceed their purpose in life.

POWERIDEA

I define *personal success* as something that you have enough passion to develop skill for and that generates legal income.

Wouldn't that make your job infinitely easier? Students with a purpose for learning persist longer on a boring task rather than give in to a tempting alternative. Students with these traits improve their science and mathematics grades over several months (Yeager et al., 2014), which is a prime example of having a *high why*. However, while all whys are still beneficial, more self-oriented or selfish motives for learning do not consistently produce the same results (Yeager et al., 2014).

I have seen self-transcendence or *high whys* up close. Every four years, I have an opportunity to go on a mission trip to build schools in Uganda. Compared to students in the United States, rarely do most Ugandan students see plentiful examples of the benefits of education. Yet for some reason, these students revere education and their teachers. They persevere to study and learn through enormous odds.

On my last trip to Uganda, I listened to journalists interview students after they registered impressive results on national examinations. The journalists wanted to know what motivated the students to work hard in their studies and pass their exams. Their responses pointed at the why of their learning. For some, the purpose that drove their learning included the problems they have grown up witnessing in their societies that they wish to solve. Others grew up watching family members, friends, and others die of curable diseases. Rather than becoming discouraged, these students promised their families they would work hard in school to become medical experts and save their communities from high and early mortality (Chen, 2014).

In a story published by the National Association of Independent Schools (Wehner, 2022), three students at a Baltimore school came up with the concept of building a hydroponic greenhouse within the campus. After the original greenhouse was destroyed, they created an urban hydroponics program in collaboration with other area schools. These students used real ideas to solve real problems!

Social inequalities impact students differently at a personal level. In my observation, students who have seen their parents survive on odd jobs, going for days on end without the basic necessities of life, tend to have an almost divine push to learn, with the hope of graduating and compensating their parents for their times of trouble. Occasionally, I hear of a student who promises a parent that they will work hard in school so that they can secure a decent future and fulfill their childhood desire of providing decent housing, food, clothing, and other luxuries for the family. When this kind of why—to alleviate poverty-stricken families from their anguish—drives students, they often go through the learning process in a distinct manner. For some students, the push to learn starts with natural gifts and passions discovered early in life and the influence of role models and personal mentors who support the students in self-discovery and plant the seed of purposeful living (Popoff, n.d.).

The benefit of possessing a powerful and personal why does not just begin in kindergarten and end after the twelfth grade; most great accomplishments in life need a why. For example, John Stephen Akhwari, a native of Tanzania in East Africa, took part in a 42-kilometer race in the 1968 Summer Olympics in Mexico City. During the marathon, he injured his shoulder and dislocated his knee after colliding with another marathoner and falling (Olympics YouTube Channel, 2021).

One hour after the winner was declared, a bloody and bandaged Akhwari pressed on to finish the race in front of a standing ovation from the few thousands of fans who were still at the stadium. When asked why he had endured the pain, the then 30-year-old athlete replied, "My country did not send me 5,000 miles to start the race; they sent me 5,000 miles to finish the race" (as cited in Olympics YouTube Channel, 2021).

How beautiful that must have been! To know his purpose and to live by it, no matter the hurdles that came his way!

When Students Don't Know Their *High Why*

How motivated or engaged can a student be if they don't have a parental push or a personal purpose driving them to endure sometimes boring material or the high expectations of learning mathematics, science, or English language arts? As the engaged students arrive at school filled with family purpose or their personal *high why*, the biggest danger we face is that the partially engaged and disengaged students may come to school without a *high why* and not find it in school either. Because if they don't find their *high why* at home or in school, they could easily conclude that the main purpose for engaging in schoolwork is blind obedience or simply to avoid penalties.

Sadly, what happens if a student concludes that home and school penalties no longer matter? The natural next steps most likely are disengagement, disruption, self-destruction, or maybe dropping out. A study on student dropouts identifies the following factors that contribute to students not finding or possessing their *high why* (Blazer & Gonzalez Hernandez, 2018).

- Lack of relevant curriculum
- Shortage of opportunities for active learning
- Disregard of students' individual learning styles

- Low expectations for student achievement
- Lack of adequate counseling
- Unfair disciplinary policies
- Lack of positive and trusting relationships with school staff
- Number of family responsibilities
- Lack of family support

Isn't it regrettable that students often go through education cycles unaware of who they are and why they go through schooling? I often feel that students are caught between a rock and a hard place. On the one hand, educators must push students to meet the high expectations of federal and state requirements, while on the other hand, parents push them to attend and behave whether they understand the purpose for education or not! As the students' classroom coach, you can change that by helping students identify a purpose for learning. A purpose that they will share in their household, with their peers, and ultimately with the world. To help students think about the process, I created the BEST system. I simply asked students to always do their BEST to discover their best self. The following was on my classroom wall, and my students often repeated it as a reminder of my classroom philosophy.

B: Be prepared to always do your best, because responsibilities are opportunities to discover your abilities!

E: Expose yourself to life, because if you can't see it, how can you be it?

S: Serve your community, because no one is an island unto themselves!

T: Test yourself to know what you can do.

I encourage you to create a strategy to begin building an unbreakable relationship with your students by becoming a valuable member of their dream team and helping each student find their *high why* for learning and living.

To help your students begin to understand why they need your class and why they need to do well, use the reproducible "Why I Need These Classes" on page 58. It will also help you start the conversation to convince students to own their learning. In other words, they are not learning just to get a grade from you; they are learning to achieve their goals and become the person they want to become, which will help them realize their own *high why*. Next, we will explore the importance of fostering cooperative competition in classrooms.

What Type of Person Do You Want to Be?

Directions: Forty years from today, you are receiving an award for achieving personal success. The spokesperson comes to the podium to talk about the great things you have done. What do they say about you? (Check each box that you agree with.)

Family
- ☐ I am married, and I have children.
- ☐ I am not married and have no children.
- ☐ I am a loving parent, and I am not married.
- ☐ I am married, and my children have their own home and careers.
- ☐ I am a loving and generous partner.

Education
- ☐ I achieved personal success by graduating from college and getting a good job.
- ☐ I achieved personal success by starting my own business.
- ☐ I achieved personal success by going to trade school or the military.

Character
- ☐ I am trustworthy and do not steal or cheat.
- ☐ I am respectful and considerate of others.
- ☐ I am responsible, self-controlled, and self-disciplined.

Caring
- ☐ I care for the less fortunate, and I am kind to others.
- ☐ I help my school by reading to first-grade kids.
- ☐ I volunteer coach for my daughter's soccer team.

Community
- ☐ I am a leader in my community.
- ☐ I help students in my neighborhood in their schools.
- ☐ I give to the poor in my community.
- ☐ I am a good citizen and a good person in my community.

Why I Need These Classes

Directions: Based on the type of person that you want to become, how does each class help you win in life?

Name: _____ Grade: _____ Date: _____

My Class	How It Helps Me Win in Life	My Current Grade
Mathematics		
English		
Social Studies		
History		
Science		

CHAPTER 6

Power Move: Foster Cooperative Competition

Alone we can do so little. Together we can do so much.

—Helen Keller

When I was a kid, I hated eating squash. Whenever my parents put squash on my plate, I closed my eyes, and with a child's imagination, I believed that it would be gone when I opened my eyes. It never worked. The squash was always there. I still had to eat it.

Some facts are like squash. Whether we like them or not, they are facts, and they are not going away. One such fact is that life is competitive, and competition is life. Whether we like competition or not, our students must compete and learn from it. However, competition doesn't have to be painful or evil. It can be healthy, like my squash. Unlike my squash, competition can be fun, and everyone can win if students cooperate to achieve a mutually beneficial goal.

This chapter explores the differences between healthy and unhealthy competition and introduces the concept of cooperative competition. Then, we discuss cooperative competition by going through an example of improving students' reading. Finally, we will learn why competitive grit can help students in school and as adults.

Healthy and Unhealthy Competition

When I say *competition* to teachers during training sessions or workshops, what most have internalized that to mean is similar to the Wikipedia definition (n.d.): "Competition is a rivalry where two or more parties strive for a common goal that cannot be shared: where one's gain is the other's loss." In this definition, the fact that there are winners and losers means the losing students feel inferior, while winning students feel superior, which leads to unhealthy competition. However, there is another way to compete, and real-life competition can be healthy and beneficial for all. Because when competition is cooperative, competition can be healthy. I call this *cooperative competition.*

POWERIDEA

When competition is cooperative, competition can be healthy. I call this *cooperative competition.*

Cooperative learning is not new to educators, and it is a powerful method for preparing students for real-world work environments. One definition of *cooperative learning* is the instructional use of small groups so that students work together to maximize their own and each other's learning (Johnson, Johnson, & Smith, 2014).

Healthy competition using cooperation offers tremendous benefits. For example, in a study on competition in Canada, teachers who participated observed that competition "motivates the students to get their work done and do a good job" (Goegan & Daniels, 2022). At the intersection of cooperation and competition is where the real power lies. In the world of work that we prepare our students for, this powerful combination is referred to as *co-opetition.* Professors Adam Brandenburger and Barry Nalebuff (2021) explain it by saying that co-opetition is "cooperating with a competitor to achieve a common goal or get ahead." One great example of this is our goal to explore space.

There was always fierce competition between the United States and Russia. However, in 1975 under the leadership of then President Gerald Ford, there was a deal to cooperate with the then-Soviet Union to work together on Apollo-Soyuz, and by 1998 the jointly managed International Space Station had ushered in an era of co-opetition. Now the practice is common in a wide range of industries, having been adopted by rivals such as Apple and Samsung, DHL and UPS, Ford and General Motors, and Google and Yahoo (Brandenburger & Nalebuff, 2021).

Furthermore, research from New York University on competition highlights that it also increases student interest in the learning process even in difficult subjects (Games and Learning, 2014). The following are some key findings from the study.

- Students playing competitively solved 45 percent more mathematics problems than those playing by themselves.

- Students reported enjoying the game more when they played competitively (19 percent increase) or collaboratively (20 percent increase).

- All students improved their mathematics skills after playing the game, no matter whether they played competitively or not (Games and Learning, 2014).

Competition can encourage students to reflect on their lessons and understand how to apply learned content, and it can create a team atmosphere that strengthens relationships.

Cooperative Competition in Practice

As a coach and a teacher, I have long understood how cooperation and competition can work together. I hypothesized that teachers could use the benefits of cooperative learning and competition to build relationships and increase student engagement. In multiple school districts, I tested the benefits of cooperative competition in the classroom to increase student motivation and teacher-student engagement. In each instance, the results were phenomenal. The goal is not to focus on learning outcomes but on the process of learning that leads students to the outcomes.

The first time I applied this idea of cooperative competition was as a school leader at the Male Leadership Academy in Charlotte, North Carolina. The second time was with the third-grade students and staff at Burton Glen Charter Academy in Burton, Michigan. Each time, cooperative competition became a bridge for students who benefited from the organic camaraderie with other students. Additionally, it became a bridge for teachers to create relationships and increase student and family engagement.

In the case of Burton Glen Charter Academy, teachers experienced attendance and behavioral issues with students due to the huge engagement gap. They theorized this engagement gap was also the source of unnecessary confrontations with parents. If this were true, this gap or disconnect might be affecting academic results. I shared with them the research, my experience, and the connection between teacher-student relationships and academic performance, and then suggested that we test the cooperative competition strategy. An added motivation to try something new was the school leader's desire to promote higher academic scores to families so that the school could better compete for enrollment in the fall. Therefore, the staff decided to try it with seventy-eight third-grade students to prepare them for the upcoming winter NWEA MAP reading test. The teachers used an online assessment tool for weekly progress monitoring. They also wanted to get parents engaged and students motivated to do their best and stay focused for the test.

The students in each class—not the teacher—picked a name for the class team. Then the competition began. There are three levels of cooperative competition: (1) personal success, (2) team success, and (3) class celebration, plus an optional bonus level of (4) intra-competition. The following sections highlight the school's experience and progression through the levels.

Level 1: Personal Success

To start, each student competed against their reading scores from the previous week. Goal setting is a precious skill for students that helps them answer current problems while building confidence to go after long-term solutions, such as their lifetime ambitions.

Third-grade readers should be reading 114 words per minute (wpm), so if a student read 100 wpm one week, the teacher and the student set a greater wpm goal and strategy for the following week. That goal would be the student's personal success goal, and it represented the number of points they would score for their class team. To help determine a student's personal success goal for a competition in your classroom, use the reproducible "Personal Success Goal Sheet" on page 67 for each student. This will also give you an exciting opportunity to meet with each student to discuss their current performance and agree on possibilities and expectations.

Level 2: Team Success

We added up each student's personal success goal score, which resulted in the class's aggregate score and team goal. The class as a team competed to meet or beat the class aggregate score or achieve a certain percentage of class growth as determined by the teacher. The beauty of this procedure is that every student, regardless of their level of competence, can participate and help the team win. Because lower-performing students have more ground to make up, they often score more personal success points than high-performing students do.

Level 3: Class Celebration

Students celebrated achieving their personal success goals, and the entire class celebrated achieving or beating its aggregate and team goal, or the progress made toward their goal. Our motto was, "We win as a team, we lose as a team." There were no individual losers or winners. When we won, we celebrated it with dress-down days or extra time outside. For big victories, we would take a field trip to the students' place of choice (within reason). Meeting with each student to discuss possibilities and expectations and to set individual contributions helped to ensure a victory. However, on the rare chance a classroom did not hit their number, we intentionally turned our attention to celebrating effort, teamwork, and our next opportunity. It also gave us a reason to have a group discussion about real-world cooperative consequences where we reinforced that no one is an island unto themselves.

Level 4: Intra-Competition (Bonus Level)

Multiple classrooms on the same level can compete against each other's aggregate or team classroom scores, which is when the real engagement fun starts! As expected, Burton Glen Charter Academy achieved similar results to the Male Leadership Academy. The following is a summary of their outcomes.

- At level 1, personal success, students were excited to meet or beat their personal success scores in reading from the previous week, which motivated students and provided a vehicle for increased teacher-student and family engagement around positive academic issues. In one week, the online assessment tool reported that 18 percent of students increased their wpm by four or more words. Most of the increase came from previously lower-performing students. Fifty-nine percent of students improved by two to three wpm, 15 percent improved by one wpm (higher-performing students), and 8 percent of students had no gain.

- At level 2, team success, all students in the class were on the same team and involved in healthy academic competition to meet or beat their class's aggregate goal. Each student knew that they could contribute and benefit the whole. Therefore, students beat their class aggregate goal because more students exceeded their personal success wpm goal. Additionally, they met their class percentage goal of 90 percent of the students increasing their word knowledge in one week.

At the end of the competition, students said they were more confident in their reading abilities. Teachers said they enjoyed the process and benefited from their newfound relationships with students and parents—relationships built on academic performance.

From my experiences with these schools, I can verify that competition works when educators implement it correctly. Cooperative competition adds fun and excitement to the classroom and is one of the most powerful tools a teacher or a school can use. As mentioned earlier, this is primarily because it fuels student motivation and drives teacher-student engagement.

Competitive Grit

With the noted benefits, educators should embrace healthy competition in K–12 by following a few straightforward suggestions. I have found these helpful for structuring competitive practices that aid in engagement and all-around development in students.

- Ensure that the prize's value is of little importance (even if donated by parents), to make sure that students are intrinsically motivated. Which is important because I discovered that the perceived value of the gift drove my students' efforts instead of personal gratification or the process itself. Focusing on the process rather than on the prize helps students to avoid engaging in dishonest practices. Of course, even this is not foolproof for students, but paying attention to this tip will increase your participation and success.

- Keep the duration of the competition short. A long-term competition can cause stress to mount on students over time, leading to demotivation.

- Do your best to keep it fun and, as young people say, "Keep it hyped." One of the ways I did this was to ask students (in the hallway, classroom, lunchroom, and so on), "How many points you got for me this week?" I followed their answer with a high-five, and I told them that, "I know you got it in you, because teamwork makes the dream work!"

- Give all students a chance to win. Otherwise, learned helplessness (trying without ever winning) removes the incentive to try.

- Emphasize that learning and improving is winning. Celebrate effort and improvement.

We live in a highly competitive society, which is the world our students will enter someday. We need to teach students to bounce back from failure, respond positively to challenges, and handle defeat. In addition, we need to teach them the power of effort. If we don't teach them to have the passion and perseverance that psychologist Angela Duckworth (2016) talks about in her book *Grit: The Power of Passion and Perseverance*, we set students up for future failure and dissatisfaction.

One of the profound findings in Duckworth's seminal research was how grit was a predictor of who would make it to and through the United States Military Academy at West Point. West Point has an enrollment process that requires the following.

- Top scores on the SAT or ACT
- Outstanding high school grades
- Applications submitted starting in eleventh grade
- Nomination from a congressperson, senator, or vice president of the United States
- A fitness assessment that includes running, push-ups, sit-ups, and pull-ups

Each year more than 14,000 applicants begin the process of applying to West Point. Only 4,000 receive the required nomination. Only 2,500 meet West Point's academic and physical standards. Finally, only 1,200 ultimately enroll. Although many West Point students were high school varsity athletes (most were team captains), only 960 graduate from the Academy. Why is that?

One factor that separates those who graduate from those who don't is their level of grit. Duckworth writes that:

> In summary, no matter the category, the highly successful had a kind of ferocious determination that played out in two ways. First, these exemplars were usually resilient and hardworking. Second, they knew in very, very deep ways what it was they wanted. It was this combination of passion and perseverance that made high achievers special. In a word they had grit. (Duckworth, 2016, p. 8)

The West Point example shows us that not only do we need to help students learn how to succeed, but we also need to help them learn how to fail forward. It is wise to acknowledge our students who live and survive the horrors attached to poverty and recognize that in spite of the traumas that they experience, the mere fact that they are in school is a triumph. Also, the fact that they continue with their education in spite of all that they experience demonstrates grit. Healthy competition while learning accomplishes that goal. Cooperative competition can help students develop and increase their grit in a safe environment. Just as importantly, competition helps students be mentally and emotionally prepared for future success and possible failures, both professionally and socially.

Competition Concerns

Those concerned about students competing often highlight the negatives associated with competition, including heightened student anxiety and fear of failure. Therefore, some schools are choosing multiple valedictorians to avoid the possible downsides of competitive practices. Also, some schools now announce from fifty to one-hundred valedictorians to prevent self-esteem issues (Howard, 2015). If we are not careful, we will be on the road to eliminating competition in school. There's a considerable disadvantage in eliminating competition from our classrooms.

The modern-day innovation that suggests we teach students that everyone is a winner has me concerned that we will lead students to a place where they are not ready to deal with life's realities. The reality is that sometimes on your best day, with your best efforts, you will not take home the trophy. Sometimes your best effort does not get you the job. These are realities in life for all of us, but we give our best while expecting the best.

POWERIDEA

The modern-day innovation that suggests we teach students that everyone is a winner will lead us to a bad place, a place where students are not ready to deal with life's realities.

"We want to encourage effort, especially among young kids," says psychologists Jean M. Twenge and W. Keith Campbell, authors of *The Narcissism Epidemic: Living in the Age of Entitlement.* "But the 'everybody gets a trophy' mentality basically says that you're going to get rewarded just for showing up. That won't build true self-esteem; instead, it builds this empty sense of 'I'm just fantastic, not because I did anything but just because I'm here'" (as cited in Sigman, 2012).

As adults, students will compete with others to get a scholarship, job, or promotion. Therefore, exposing students to competition early in a loving, supportive environment provides us as educators a powerful opportunity to guide their learning process and teach them the right way to respond to failure. We can teach students to develop a thick skin and teach them the courage to persist despite temporary or seemingly permanent setbacks. We can also teach them that, while they should aspire and strive to win, losing should not be dreaded or avoided at all costs.

Teachers should guide engagement in classroom competition so that students understand its relevance and, as such, are less likely to sacrifice learning opportunities for better performance. Let's use cooperative competition to build grit, improve teacher-student relationships, and increase student engagement. Next, we will explore some ideas for educating and celebrating parents as partners.

Personal Success Goal Sheet

Directions: Fill out a Personal Success Goal Sheet for each student.

Name: _____ Start Date: _____ End Date: _____

Subject: _____

My current personal success performance points: _____

My future personal success performance point goal: _____

_____

_____

_____

My personal success strategies to achieve my goal:

1. I will _____

   _____

   _____

   _____

2. I will _____

   _____

   _____

   _____

3. I will _____

   _____

   _____

   _____

Number of Points Scored for My Team: _____

CHAPTER 7

Power Move: Educate and Celebrate Parents as Partners

In schools where parent involvement is greater, you do have higher achievement levels and better functioning, better performing schools.
—Michelle Rhee

Every classroom coach needs an assistant coach. Someone who cares and shows concern about students as much as you do, if not more. Someone whose concern goes beyond compensation. Someone whose sole responsibility is to provide support, resources, and labor on students' behalf. I nominate parents for the assistant coach position.

Typically, when looking for additional resources, educators go to the district for help or pay for these resources themselves. But one of the most powerful resources they have for school transformation is at their fingertips and is free. That resource is the student's family.

To explain why parents are important to educators, let me share a story that has deeply influenced me in my work with parents and my trainings with parent liaisons in schools. After one of my Power Parenting workshops, a parent approached me and shared a personal story (which I've kept anonymous here) that I have never forgotten:

> I have only one son, and I was determined to fulfill my duty as his mother to ensure he succeeds. When he was young, I had this idea he must be a lawyer.

So, from the time that he was in primary school until he entered University of Michigan Law School, I was nagging him. All the time, I pushed him to work harder and harder and told him, "You must become a lawyer. You better study hard, you better do this, you better go for this scholarship and that scholarship." But I never asked him what he wanted.

Well, I succeeded. He's now a lawyer, but he no longer talks to me! I got a lawyer, but I lost a son.

I have shared her story hundreds of times, and I still feel her pain, anguish, and regret. While her intentions were honorable, she mistakenly left out one of her greatest allies and partners for fulfilling her mission—teachers. As parents, we can have blind spots related to our children's assets and liabilities. Input from teachers provides us with a more holistic assessment of our children's purpose and passions.

However, teachers often overlook the power and influence that parents have over their children. Too often, educators make the same mistake as parents. We leave out one of our greatest allies and partners in fulfilling our mission—parents. From the age of five, students spend only about 18 percent of their total waking hours at school from kindergarten through high school, which means they spend 82 percent of their time at home or out of school. Therefore, we must recognize and respect the positive or negative influence that parents have on learning.

POWERIDEA

Students spend 82 percent of their time at home or out of school. Therefore, we must recognize and respect the positive or negative influence that parents have on learning.

Additionally, teachers do not merely deliver information to students. One could say they have a co-parenting or co-developing relationship with families. Therefore, teachers should consider that helping students succeed requires a healthy home-school partnership. I have always seen healthy home-school partnership as the ability of both parties to respectfully work together toward one goal: student development. I intentionally use the term *student development* and not *student achievement* because student achievement seems one-dimensional and only focused on academics. Therefore, I use the term student development because my concern is about first developing the child, and then achievement will follow.

However, this concept applies to students from homes where the student's family has the will to be involved and only needs compassion, opportunity, and guidance to be engaged. Students from homes with extreme poverty, substance abuse, or abandonment require another level of support. Classroom teachers should provide this support but also cannot take full accountability. What I mean by another level of support is when students come from situations with extreme poverty, substance abuse, or abandonment, it is easy to consider reasons why you would alter your expectations. At this time, your expectations can't change, but how you support students in meeting their expectations can change. Assignments that require internet access at home and certain technology may need to be reconsidered or completed at school. Field trips that require parental signature may require alternative communication to acquire the signature. Expectations don't change, but methods may.

This chapter defines parental engagement and explores the three steps for improving parental engagement: (1) clarifying how partnership means engagement, (2) educating parents, and (3) celebrating parents as partners.

Define Parental Engagement

Because students spend most of their time outside of school, parental engagement is key. However, parental involvement or engagement was probably one of the most critical but underused components of Title I in the Elementary and Secondary Education Act (ESEA) since it became law in 1965. Amazingly, ESEA never defined parental involvement until the 2001 reauthorization of the act. This amendment clarified the term *parental involvement* and lawfully established that parents are the key stakeholders in their children's education. The definition of parent and parental involvement is in Section 9101 of the ESEA:

> (31) PARENT- The term 'parent' includes a legal guardian or other person standing in loco parentis (such as a grandparent or stepparent with whom the child lives, or a legally responsible person for the child's welfare).

> (32) PARENTAL INVOLVEMENT- The term 'parental involvement' means the participation of parents in regular, two-way, and meaningful communication involving student academic learning and other school activities, including ensuring—

> (A) that parents play an integral role in assisting their child's learning;

> (B) that parents are encouraged to be actively involved in their child's education at school; that parents are full partners in their child's education and are included, as appropriate, in decision making and on advisory committees to assist in the education of their child;

> (C) the carrying out other activities, such as those described in section 1118.
> (U.S. Department of Education, 2014, p. 31)

While it's important to have this national definition, it is essential for school districts inside or outside the United States to have their own local definition for parent involvement that does not exclude or conflict with the national definition. The local definition should be more precise and define parent involvement or engagement requirements for stakeholders. It also shapes the expectations for all new families. The partnering process can begin once the school district has established a local definition.

To help schools begin to create a culture of parent partnership, I regularly walk school districts through the three-step partnership process outlined in this chapter's introduction. This process (1) clarifies the parent's role (that partnership means engagement), (2) educates the parents, and (3) celebrates the engagement of parent partners, culminating in a completion certificate for the parents. For an example of its efficacy, out of 288 schools, Burton Glen Charter Academy in Burton, Michigan, won several school engagement awards from their college authorizer Central Michigan University and management company National Heritage Academies with the help of this process.

The goal and expectation of the process is to build a parent partnership tipping point in the parent culture and set parents and teachers on fire for engagement. The back cover of Malcolm Gladwell's book *The Tipping Point* (2002) brilliantly describes this *tipping point* phenomenon as:

> That magic moment when an idea, trend, or social behavior crosses a threshold, tips, and spreads like wildfire. Just as a single sick person can start an epidemic of the flu, so too can a small but precisely targeted push cause a fashion trend, the popularity of a new product, or a drop in the crime rate.

The following sections walk you through how the three-step certificate partnership process works to tip parents from being interested observers to being involved partners in their child's education.

Clarify That Partnership Means Engagement

We cannot assume parents know what engagement is, why it's important, or how to engage with their child's school or teacher. When I begin working with a new school, I often find that one of two scenarios exist for parents who want to be involved and engaged: (1) parents find themselves discouraged because they are just being told what to do, or (2) parents are frustrated by lack of a definition for what school partnership should look like. Unfortunately, not many schools or districts have clarified their local definition for parent partnership.

The school or district may have a mission statement, but it also needs a statement of core values or parenting ethos. Educators and researchers Richard DuFour, Rebecca DuFour, Robert Eaker, and Thomas Many (2010) explain that a core value statement clarifies how we must behave to make our shared vision a reality. Without this clarity for local parent partnership, it's difficult to speak frankly or share qualitative data about parents in the district. Without a parent partnership core value statement for a local district or building, each stakeholder defaults to their own definition of parent involvement.

Also during this step, we make the critical distinction between involvement and engagement. Too often, we only want parents to be involved in the agendas and activities that we establish, without their input. However, involvement alone is not engagement and, therefore, not partnership.

Therefore, I recommend making a clear distinction between involvement and engagement. This clarification is so important that Philadelphia School District's Office of Family and Community Engagement formally clarified these two terms for its district.

> "Family involvement" and "family engagement" are not one in the same. These are two very distinct concepts that look different in practice and yield different outcomes and results. A definition of "involve" is "to enfold or envelope;" conversely, "engage" can be defined as "to come together and interlock." Thus, involvement implies doing-to, whereas engagement implies doing-with. (The School District of Philadelphia, 2021)

Fostering engagement over involvement may initially seem like a lot of work. Or you may be somewhat uncomfortable truly engaging with students' families. But what you are doing is gaining another set of eyes, ears, and hands to help you accomplish your goals. An investment in engaging with parents will magnify your results and make dozens of things easier and more effective down the road.

Schools and districts need to set the meaningful minimum engagement expectations for parents to be considered a partner in this school or district. *Meaningful minimums* are the foundational tasks that, if parents consistently complete them, their child will have an improved chance of succeeding. These tasks can change from district to district, but they must be tasks that consider the socioeconomic and geographical makeup of parents locally. For instance, if your district serves a population that largely does not have internet access at home, it wouldn't be wise to create a meaningful minimum that requires students to complete homework assignments that require research and home printing. However, if one of your meaningful minimums is for parents to check their child's academic progress in your school information system, then internet access is probably not a huge issue, as most families will be able to access it on their cell phone app.

Keeping everyone focused on meaningful minimums is important in this first step, because if you're not careful, you will create barriers to partnerships. It's not the time to think about what you would do as a parent or to develop an exclusive parent club. Think about the requirements parents in your school could and should meet to achieve the meaningful minimum. This step is about building bridges, not barriers.

Educate Parents

Clarifying the partnership prepares you for this step, which moves to educating and training parents on how to engage with teachers and schools so you can have quantitative data of the home-school partnership. When I work with instructional teams, I ask, "How many parents do you currently believe are in partnership with your school?" Once we settle on a number, I follow up with, "How do you know that to be accurate?" Too often, their number is derived from personal experience. I realized that schools need a method to identify and quantify the parents and families who were truly in partnership with them.

With the help of several schools, I researched, developed, implemented, and tested a course called Power Parenting. Details about the course can be found at www.PowerParentingU.com. It consists of seven modules for parents and proved to be a powerful program on meaningful minimums. Schools can use this system to target a small group of parents, such as their parent leadership group, begin with a targeted grade level, or launch it schoolwide. Participating parents can go online with their school code and learn about the basic strategies for partnering with their child's school. When implemented and promoted with fidelity, simply signing up and then completing the seven-module course demonstrates a family's willingness to partner and engage. The completion of the course also provides data about which parents are engaged and have been educated on meaningful minimums.

Over the years, this partnership course has increased home-school partnerships by 30 percent. The measured benefits of these partnerships have been most significant in the areas of student attendance and behavior. Of the more than 100 schools that have used the system, Burton Glen Charter Academy is the best example because of the school leaders' buy-in, which signaled to others the project's priority and influenced the fidelity with which their school team implemented the system.

The seven Power Parenting course modules that educate and train parents to be partners with their child's school are the following.

1. **The power of home expectations:** Parents learn the power of setting high expectations at home and supporting the high expectations of teachers at school.

2. **The power of attendance:** Parents learn the powerful connection between attendance and academic achievement.

3. **The power of rest:** Parents learn they have the power and responsibility to ensure their child has a good night's sleep. They are given medical facts on the connection between sleep and academic performance.

4. **The power of home-school communication:** Parents learn they have the power and responsibility to ensure consistent and meaningful communication with their child's school.

5. **The power of volunteering:** Parents learn how volunteering not only benefits their child but also supports all students in the building.

6. **The power of homework:** Parents learn the powerful benefits of monitoring homework and how to connect life experiences to assignments.

7. **The power of school and community leadership:** Parents learn the power of being part of an action-oriented, problem-solving network of parent partners who are active in PTAs and other groups.

With the help of the school and teachers, parents learn strategies for seven research-based meaningful minimums to help them better engage with their child's school and be able to help their child succeed. These seven meaningful minimum strategies are not based on socioeconomic situations or skill. They are based on families' willpower to help and engage. Therefore, for those parents who have the willpower to support their child at school, this program helps them learn as they get involved and engaged.

Let's look at what I consider the foundational four of the seven engagement meaningful minimums. These first four modules are foundational because every family has the ability and responsibility to complete these four of the seven. It is important that most of your parents accept their responsibility for these first four modules, so I will unpack them in the following sections. The final three are self-explanatory and for those parents who want to go above and beyond.

The Power of Home Expectations

The first module helps parents understand the value of setting expectations for their children at home. This training helps them appreciate their influence and role in preparing their child for the classroom, academically and behaviorally. Unfortunately, this is a secret weapon that most parents and teachers don't use.

In this module, parents learn how family expectations in kindergarten can predict student's own expectations for postsecondary educational attainment (Froiland, 2013). It's essential that parental expectations are reasonable and achievable, so they don't backfire and lead to more stress than success. This module can help families consider how they want to communicate their academic and behavioral philosophy to their children. Will it be through rewards, punishment, or a combination of both? This is also a time for parents to evaluate teachers' expectations of their children and recognize the value of mirroring those expectations as best they can.

In this module, parents discover that setting the expectation for learning should be a basic prerequisite in their parenting toolbox. Most importantly, having dreams and expectations doesn't cost anything. Regardless of their socioeconomic status, all parents can meet this meaningful minimum expectation. To help set meaningful minimum requirements, use the reproducible "Set Meaningful Minimum Expectations" on page 80.

The Power of Attendance

This module establishes the power of presence. As a school principal, I always made it clear to my parents at orientation that success started with being at school, then being at school on time, and then being at school on time and ready to learn every day. These criteria create a powerful meaningful minimum. While chronic absenteeism is an obvious problem, parents also need to learn the facts behind the data. Whenever their child is absent from or late to classes in a high-performing environment, it's even harder for them to catch up. Which is especially true in sequential classes such as mathematics or science, where many objectives and lessons depend on having mastered previous skills.

Research is helping us understand that absenteeism poses a problem as early as kindergarten and beyond high school. A major report, *Chronic Absenteeism: A Research Review* (Brooks, DeJong, Lytton, Pacheco, & Pradhan, 2020), defines *chronic absenteeism* as missing 10 percent of school or more for any reason, including excused, unexcused, and disciplinary absences. Here are some important findings from the report that educators and parents need to know (Brooks et al., 2020).

- Over seven million U.S. students were chronically absent from school in 2015–2016

- More than 20 percent of high school students are chronically absent

- More than 14 percent of middle school students are chronically absent

- Almost 14 percent of elementary school students are chronically absent

- Twenty-five percent of kindergarten students are chronically absent or at risk of being chronically absent

Some parents don't appreciate the importance of early learning, so absenteeism is high even in kindergarten and lower grades. Help parents understand that they can't wait until high school to be concerned about attendance. While families in lower socioeconomic areas face multiple challenges that can impact attendance, such as a lack of transportation, the federal government and local schools often have resources to support parents. For example, some schools in the United States offer bus vouchers for families who may be struggling financially. Where there are clusters of families who struggle with transportation, schools have been known to arrange carpools by connecting parents with other parents in their neighborhood. Both strategies can be successful in lowering school absenteeism while increasing the health of the home-school relationship. Schools need to make families aware of these resources so families can be empowered to prioritize attendance. Another noteworthy point from the report is that absenteeism is not particular to either gender; roughly 16 percent of male and female students are similarly likely to be chronically absent.

The Power of Rest

In this module, parents learn the importance of setting structured times for their children to sleep. While our childhoods are never quite as simple as we like to remember as adults, I know for myself and many in my generation that life certainly seemed simpler. The community I lived in had informal agreements about how a child's day would be, and most children followed the same routine. Our parents woke us up in the morning, we waited our turn for the bathroom, ate breakfast, and then walked to school with our friends. After school, we walked home, had a snack, and did our homework. If the weather was nice (enough), after our parents made sure we finished our tasks, we went outside to play with the mandate to be in before the streetlights turned on. Once back inside, we washed up, had dinner with the family, and watched TV with our family because it was the only TV in the house. After watching TV, we laid out our school clothes and went to bed. This routine or some version of it happened the same way every day for countless kids until summertime. Those were the days.

Modern students don't always have that much predictability or structure in their lives. Many spend their days consumed with phone calls and screen time, either from TV, computers, or cell phones, which can continue long into the night. Because of this routine, their sleep patterns are very different from those of their parents or grandparents. However, their bodies have not changed. Children today still need the same amount of sleep as I did when I was growing up. Unfortunately, many modern students arrive at school sleep deprived. According to the Centers for Disease Control:

> Insufficient sleep among children and adolescents is associated with an increased risk for obesity, diabetes, injuries, poor mental health, attention and behavior problems, and poor academic performance. Nationwide, approximately two thirds of U.S. high school students report sleeping [fewer than] 8 hours per night on school nights. (Wheaton, Jones, Cooper, & Croft, 2018) Whether we like it or not, students who do not have structured sleep times uninterrupted by technology arrive each day to school and have a harder time paying attention, remember less, and are not as quick to make associations with relevant ideas, making it harder for them to learn (Wheaton, Jones, Cooper, & Croft, 2018).

A multidisciplinary expert panel, along with the National Sleep Foundation (Hirshkowitz, Whiton, Albert, Alessi, Bruni, DonCarlos, et al., 2015), published its suggestions for proper sleep times. In addition, the expert panel advises longer sleep times for most age groups.

- **School-age children (ages 6–13):** Sleep range increased by one hour to nine to eleven hours (previously it was ten to eleven hours)

- **Teenagers (ages 14–17):** Sleep range increased by one hour to eight to ten hours (previously, it was eight and one-half to nine and one-half hours)

In this Power Parenting module, we arm parents with factual, scientific information about their child's need for sleep. As a result, parents walk away from this meaningful minimum with valuable information and greater sensitivity for the power of rest and how it affects their child's behavior and learning.

The Power of Home-School Communication

It's hard to believe that the people in the two places where students spend most of their time struggle to communicate. Study after study proves that effective partnerships between schools and families improve students' academic outcomes. One such study declared that "Parents' perceptions of school communication was predictive of their involvement" (Park & Holloway, 2013) However, families and educators struggle to build the relationship that can help students—especially the struggling students who need it the most. Communication is one of the most important variables in promoting positive family–school relationships (Gartmeier, Gebhardt, & Dotger, 2016).

This meaningful minimum of home-school communication is important because family engagement tends to decline across the grades unless schools and teachers implement appropriate partnership practices early and at each grade level. This module introduces parents to the definition of parent involvement as stated in ESEA Title I: "The statute defines parental involvement as the participation of parents in regular, two-way, and meaningful communication involving student academic learning and other school activities" (U.S. Department of Education, 2004, p. 3).

ESEA places a major emphasis on two-way communication. Traditionally, communication has been unidirectionally from school to home, with an occasional note or call passing information from home to school. However, healthy two-way communication must be ongoing and comprehensive because it lays the foundation for healthy relationships and engagement.

It's safe to say that honest, two-way, meaningful communication is important for any relationship to work. If a relationship is to last, communication must take place regularly. It's also safe to say that once this communication stops, the relationship either has come to or is coming to an end.

Celebrate Parents as Partners

For this final step, it is important to celebrate and show gratitude toward all parents and teachers who helped complete the partner process. This is a time to cement the home-school relationship. This certification process also begins to build a pipeline of healthy, informed volunteers who can also serve as marketing representatives in the community to increase school enrollment. It helps create a virtuous cycle of involvement and recruitment of other involved parents.

Psychologist Daniel E. Forster and colleagues Eric Pedersen, Adam Smith, Michael McCullough, and Debra Lieberman sum up their research on gratitude in this way: "Gratitude is an emotion that is typically evoked when one receives costly, unexpected, and intentionally rendered benefits, and is thought to play a key role in regulating the initiation and maintenance of social relationships" (Forster et. al, 2017, p. 18).

Muhammed (2018, p. 128) writes that: "The schools that celebrated authentically regularly created a greater atmosphere for collegiality. Collegiality is not collaboration but having colleagues who genuinely like and respect one another creates an atmosphere ripe for collaboration."

Pause and take some time alone or with your team to consider your school's unique meaningful minimums. As you develop a rough draft of your classroom meaningful minimums, consult with parents. Ask them which minimums make sense and are achievable. Listen carefully to the feedback and be prepared to adjust the minimums as the responses suggest. Moving someone from not involved to a little involved is the hardest move, and it only happens when parents feel listened to.

A word of warning. Beware of Super Parents who will live up to all the expectations and attempt to force every other parent to do the same. They might mean well, but these parents are not setting meaningful minimums. Your goal is to help every parent increase their engagement and help their students be successful in school and beyond. You don't want to judge a parenting contest.

Use the reproducibles "Set Meaningful Minimum Expectations" and "Set Meaningful Minimum Expectations at Home" (page 81) to uncover what is most important and possible for parents and families to participate in so everyone can feel engaged and have a hand in their child's success. Next, we will explore how to target your boys in the classroom and help them to succeed.

Set Meaningful Minimum Expectations

Directions: The following tool will help you create your meaningful minimums for parent engagement. Considering income, transportation, and education, what meaningful minimum expectations can you set for all families in order to increase home-school engagement?

	Family expectations	How will you communicate these expectations?	How will you celebrate families who meet them?
Academics: What are the *meaningful minimum* expectations you believe each family could and should meet regarding academic engagement?			
Behavior: What are the *meaningful minimum* expectations for supporting student behavior?			
Culture: What are the *meaningful minimum* expectations for every parent regarding their contribution to building a safe and successful culture?			
Supplemental: Are there any other *meaningful minimum* expectations that each parent should meet?			

Set Meaningful Minimum Expectations at Home

Directions: The following tool will help you create meaningful minimums for your home. Considering your resources and your desire for your child to excel in school and life, what meaningful minimum expectations can you set for yourself to increase home-school engagement?

	Family expectations	How will you communicate these expectations?	How will you celebrate at home when you meet them?
Academics: What are the *meaningful minimum* expectations you believe your family could and should meet regarding academic engagement?			
Behavior: What are the *meaningful minimum* expectations for your child's behavior at school?			
Culture: What are your *meaningful minimums* for the school to build a safe space for your child?			
Supplemental: Are there any other *meaningful minimum* expectations that you want to meet at home?			

CHAPTER 8

Power Move:
Target Your Boys

What are little boys made of?
What are little boys made of?
Snips, snails
And puppy-dogs' tails
That's what little boys are made of.

—Unknown

As a young man, I loved to roller skate. My friends and I roller skated on the weekends at USA Roller Rink from sunup to sundown. One day, my best friend Michael said, "Carlos, if you want to meet pretty girls in this neighborhood, you have got to learn to do two things." Since I wanted to meet a pretty girl, I was all ears. He said, "first you have to learn to skate backward, and then you have to learn to skate backward with a girl." I realized that he was right. I had to be able to do both of those things at the same time in order to win the heart of a pretty girl. And, yes, I learned how to do both of those things!

Now, before you look at the chapter title and skip to the next chapter, please know there is no reason that we can't do two important things at once, or as my dad used to say, chew bubblegum and walk at the same time. In other words, there is no reason that we can't highlight and correct issues affecting boys while maintaining victories and advances that we have achieved for girls. We can and must do both successfully.

As a classroom coach who cares about the unique ills that all students face regardless of ethnicity, economics, or gender, you need to know the following information.

1. Boys raised in low-income families do worse, in terms of adult outcomes, than girls raised in low-income families. Most strikingly, boys raised in families in the bottom fifth of the income distribution are less likely than girls either to be employed or to move up the income ladder once they become adults. (Reeves & Nzau, 2021).

2. In Canada, boys born in the poorest households are about twice as likely as girls to remain poor as adults (Corak, 2017).

If we are to prove to our families raising boys and to our students that we care about both boys and girls, we must highlight and correct issues affecting boys while maintaining the victories and advances that we have achieved for girls. May I suggest we start with acknowledging what we know. We know from an American Sociological Association (2016) report that behavior problems impact long-term educational attainment more for boys than girls, and that boys with the same behavior problems as girls tend to complete fewer years of schooling.

Classroom coaches also understand that some structural educational issues are unique to boys. When I became school leader for the Male Leadership Academy, I inherited young men from many schools in the surrounding area that operated with an unconscious bias against boys in grades three through eight. However, after three years, ninety-five percent of my boys experienced one year of growth, 65 percent were reading at grade level, and 10 percent grew a year and a half on our end-of-the-year assessments. Although we were all proud of the academic achievements, we were most proud that we took boys who demonstrated behavioral problems in other school districts and transformed them into young scholars who, at the very least, tolerated learning, but most of them engaged and embraced it.

In three years, we proved that boys are not inherently bad. By building healthy relationships, we discovered that even the boys seemingly with the most headwinds working against them want to engage in the learning process and can learn. However, there is a difference between boys and girls that we must acknowledge in the classroom if you target boys for learning.

This chapter explains why targeting girls worked and why disciplining boys doesn't work. Then it explores how to target boys effectively to move them toward success.

Targeting Support for Girls Works

The U.S. Congress passed the landmark Title IX of the Education Amendments of 1972 (Title IX) largely to ensure gender equality in higher education. Title IX prohibits discrimination based on gender in education programs and activities that receive federal financial assistance. The following are a few ways Title IX education changed education (Gaille, 2017).

- Before Title IX, most athletic scholarship opportunities were granted to men, and athletic scholarships for women were rare.

- In 1972, about 30,000 women participated in sports sponsored by the National Collegiate Athletics Association (NCAA). Today, more than 500,000 women participate.

- Because of Title IX, girls can take shop classes, not only home economics.

- Before 1972, student administrators could legally expel girls from schools simply because they were pregnant. Even young parents attending college could find it difficult to attend classes because of their home responsibilities.

During the next fifty years, something happened that we did not expect. By 1982, the gap between boys and girls in school vanished. By 2019, the gender gap was fifteen points wider than in 1972, but the other way around—in favor of women (National Center for Education Statistics, 2020). Girls not only closed the gender gap but also surpassed boys by fifteen points (National Center for Education Statistics, 2020).

POWERIDEA

By 1982, the gap between boys and girls in school vanished. By 2019 the gender gap was fifteen points wider than in 1972, but the other way around—in the favor of women. Girls not only closed the gender gap but also surpassed boys by fifteen points (National Center for Education Statistics, 2020).

I am not saying that Title IX single-handedly eliminated all barriers facing our girl students and the learning gaps between boys and girls. However, while we can't totally prove causation, there is a correlation between the timing of Title IX and the advancement women have made. What we do know is that, as a society, we realized that we were not being fair to women, so we passed legislation that had financial consequences for institutions that discriminated against women. In doing so, we sent a clear message to our women that the doors were open to opportunities regardless of their gender, and they walked proudly through those doors. Some may say that in the last fifty years they have knocked the doors down.

The following are three achievements from targeting our girls.

- A six percentage point gender gap in reading proficiency in the fourth grade widens to eleven percentage points by the end of the eighth grade (National Center for Education Statistics, 2019a).

- In mathematics, a six-point gap favoring boys in the fourth grade shrinks to a one-point gap by the eighth grade (National Center for Education Statistics, 2019b).

- In virtually every U.S. school district, female students outperform male students. On an ELA test, the average gap is two-thirds of a grade level and is larger than the effects of most large-scale educational interventions (Reardon, Fahle, Kalogrides, Podolsky, & Zárate, 2019).

Figure 8.1 shows that in almost all U.S. states girls lead the way at graduation time. Finally, this educational girl power trend in educational attainment is evident not just in the United States; it's global, as seen in figure 8.2 (page 88).

Ladies and gentlemen, take a bow. We have done our job well for our daughters. We identified structural barriers and biases that affected their opportunities in school and life, and then this great country responded. As I said earlier, I had to learn to not only skate backward, I had to learn to also skate backward with a partner. I had to do both. I don't believe we need more legislation, but something about our current educational model or mindset is not working for the other half of the classroom: our boys. I believe we can and must change that.

Disciplining Boys Doesn't Work

While it's tempting to start the conversation about how we can better serve our boys with a focus on instructional practices, learning strategies, and so on, I believe the best place to start is in our disciplinary practices. One could argue that we *have* targeted our boys since the 1990s, but unlike with our girls, it resulted in negative outcomes. One of the largest obstacles facing our boys is the disproportionality of discipline.

At the Male Leadership Academy, we found our boys naturally learned and thrived more in chaotic environments that presented spatial challenges than in an organized classroom model. Since far too many classroom teaching models are in favor of sitting still, talking little, and listening attentively, boys naturally struggle to comply. According to author Michael Gurian:

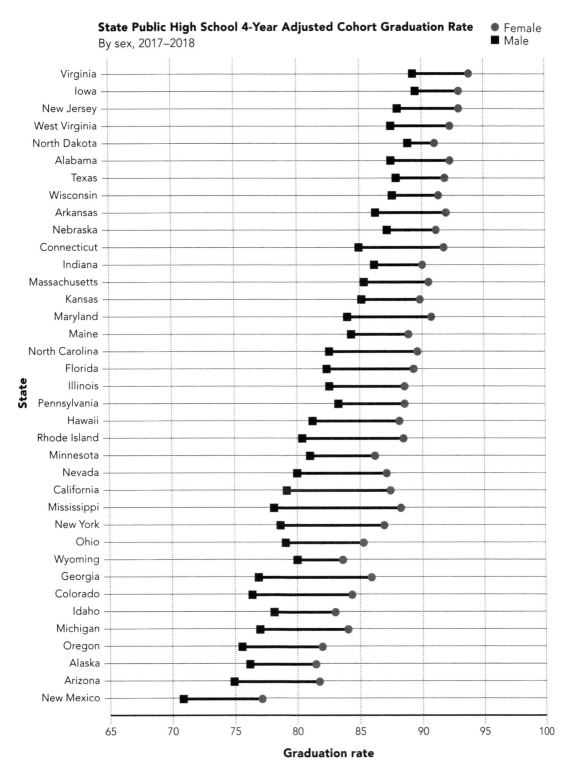

State Public High School 4-Year Adjusted Cohort Graduation Rate
By sex, 2017–2018

● Female
■ Male

Source: Reeves, Buckner, & Smith, 2021. Used with permission.

Figure 8.1: State graduation rates by sex 2017–2018.

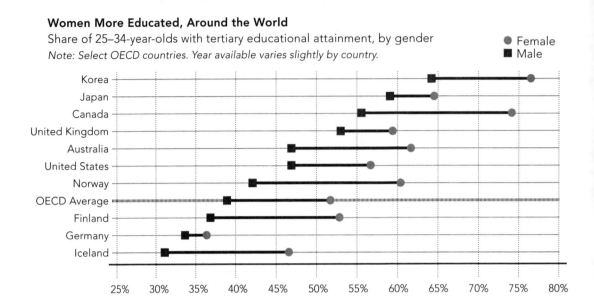

Women More Educated, Around the World
Share of 25–34-year-olds with tertiary educational attainment, by gender
Note: Select OECD countries. Year available varies slightly by country.

● Female
■ Male

Source: Reeves, 2022. Used with permission.

Figure 8.2: Country graduation rates by gender.

Males process more blood flow through the cerebellum, the 'doing' part of the brain, than females do. This biological difference may explain why boys and men are much more likely than girls and women to attach learning to movement. For boys, learning and motion go together; a boy is more likely to remember something if that information is linked to a specific movement. (as cited in Fink, 2017)

It is important to note this information is not only about boys with ADHD. What science has taught us about movement is that it's good for boys' learning. However, since many educators are unaware of the intrinsic needs of boys, boy behavior often makes them the target of discipline.

POWERIDEA

Boys in general, and more specifically Black boys, are disproportionately disciplined in K–12 public schools, according to the United States Government Accountability Office (2018).

Boys in general, and more specifically Black boys, are disproportionately disciplined in K–12 public schools, according to the United States Government Accountability Office (2018). This discipline can occur in various forms—some more detrimental than others. Certain types of disciplinary experiences, such as out-of-school suspension, can have serious consequences such as disengagement of the student and the destruction of the teacher-student relationship. Obviously, becoming a high school dropout is the final stage of the disengagement process for K–12 learning. A great presentation on this topic is the DVD *Timebomb* by Mike Mattos (Mattos, 2017).

High school dropouts and isolated young men churned out by this system are inadequately prepared for the demands of life and adulthood. As such, they often turn out to spearhead the United States' most severe social problems, incurring costs both to themselves and to society. A report released by the Center for Popular Democracy and Urban Youth Collaborative (2017), reveals the staggering yearly economic impact of the school-to-prison pipeline in New York City to be $746.8 million! These costs include the use of metal detectors and cameras, the costs of litigation and incarceration, and the school safety division.

The present educational system underserves boys in general. However, the problem is even greater with Black males because the gender differential and its effect are higher. For instance, according to Jayanti Owens (2016), assistant professor of organizational behavior at Yale School of Management, the impact of harsher discipline for boys starts as early as elementary school and, due to disengagement from boys who see school as a hostile place for them, continues from there (Owens, 2016). To help understand how discipline works in your classroom, use the reproducible "Understand Discipline in Your Classroom" on page 92.

We have to do better, and we can. Next, I will share strategies for creating healthy relationships with boys and a path to success.

Targeting Boys to Move Toward Success

We have proven since 1972 that when we put our collective minds and resources together to help a particular group, it can be done. The following is the strategy that I used to transform school culture, improve classroom behavior, and ensure that my boys were ready for the next level of performance in the classroom.

Schools across the United States have spent millions to have a police presence on campuses in the form of resource officers. We could cut that spending in half and spend the rest on resources and support that would build strong relationships between educators and students, which would be a far more effective strategy for putting boys on the right track.

There's a need to continually encourage educators to create more positive school environments. Instead of seeing our students as potential violators and criminals, we should take the human and financial resources used to service the school-to-prison pipeline and put them into creating, sustaining, and replicating a school-to-success pipeline.

My team and I created our version of a school-to-success pipeline by building a continual and contiguous support system for our young men internally through partnerships with families, community, and corporate partners. The results were phenomenal.

- In the second year of the program, 10 percent of the boys from our graduating class were accepted at and received scholarships to attend Charlotte Christian School in North Carolina, a prestigious high-performing middle school that costs $19,000 a year to attend. Before our initiative, this school was out of reach academically, behaviorally, and financially for our boys. First, there was a big cultural disconnect between our students and the Charlotte Christian School population. Second, we had to ensure that our students, if accepted, would be able to compete in the classroom. Last, even if the students could compete on the cultural and classroom level, our boys could not afford the tuition.

- Each of our third-grade boys received mentors from our college partnership with Wingate University in North Carolina. Students from the psychology department who were in their final year of study agreed to be weekly counselors. University students used a play-therapy grant that helped young boys deal with problems and trauma. As a result, the boys received valuable counseling, mentoring, and therapy once a week.

- Bank of America and Junior Achievement teamed up to provide us with a financial literacy curriculum and volunteers, which had a direct effect on our mathematics scores.

- We partnered with the Thurgood Marshall College fund to begin preparing families for opportunities to receive funding for attending historically Black colleges.

We didn't require families to participate in our school-to-success pipeline. However, those who wanted the continued and contiguous support of our growing partnerships needed to sign up for and follow our pipeline guidelines.

Our goal was simply to provide a path and a vision for our boys and their families so that they could succeed. We also wanted to assure these families that we, along with our partners, would be with them for the long journey to success. Your school or district does not need to build a pipeline exactly as we did. However, since traditional educational models have proven not to benefit the male learner enough, you can provide a living example of the level of engagement and commitment you have for their success. To help you have healthy discussions around this topic with colleagues and make data-driven decisions in your class and in your school, use the reproducible "Classroom Inventory" on page 93.

Boys need to know beyond the shadow of a doubt that you, as their classroom coach, see the problems they uniquely face and the potential in their lives and that, like any good coach, you are willing to help them develop and deliver their gifts to the world! Next, we will explore why it's important to measure student engagement frequently.

Understand Discipline in Your Classroom

Directions: Please answer the following questions.

1. What does your school discipline data look like for boys versus girls?

2. What does your classroom discipline data look like for boys versus girls?

3. What does your school discipline data look like for boys of color?

4. What does your classroom discipline data look like for boys of color?

5. In which grade do you see most of your boys having discipline problems?

6. What success programs do you have that are available for all boys?

7. What types of male mentoring programs do your school or district currently have available?

8. What percentage of your instructional team is male?

9. How has your team been trained on strategies for teaching the male brain?

Classroom Inventory

Directions: Use this tool to help you have healthy discussions with colleagues and make data-driven decisions in your class and school. Fill out the following table with the percentage of students in each ethnic category and then fill in the percentage that are proficient. Use the information to answer the reflection and respond accordingly.

	White	Black	Latino	Asian	Native American	Male	Female
Percent of school							
Reading proficiency (percent)							
Mathematics proficiency (percent)							
Percent enrolled in gifted courses							
Percent on honor roll							
Number of behavior referrals							
Percent enrolled in remedial courses							
Percent suspended at least one day							
Percent truant							
Percent with an IEP							

Reflection Questions

1. What does your data profile tell you about your classroom, grade level, or school?

2. What are your most disturbing areas? Why?

3. Hypothesize about why any visible gaps exist and how you might address them.

CHAPTER 9

Power Move: Measure Student Engagement Frequently

If you cannot measure it, you cannot improve it.

—Lord Kelvin

I love fried chicken! As an African American, I know that may sound stereotypical, but as my son would say, "It is what it is." In my pursuit of a good piece of chicken, I will occasionally go to my favorite fast-food chicken restaurant, Bojangles. However, often after waiting in line, I get to the counter and they tell me that they are out of chicken.

I always say, "How can you be out of chicken? That's what you do; you cook and sell chicken." I feel the same way when students aren't learning. I say to teachers, "This is a school; learning is what we do. How can students not be learning?" One of the biggest reasons isn't teacher incompetence. It is the lack of engagement of the student in the learning process, which is why we must measure student engagement as often as needed.

This chapter discusses three reasons for measuring student engagement: (1) to gain qualitative data; (2) to show students that you care; and (3) to track what works. Then, we explore the criteria for measuring engagement and three methods that I used at the Male Leadership Academy.

Measuring Student Engagement to Collect Qualitative Data

Formative and summative tests are great for helping teachers gather data on how much a student has learned. However, tests can't explain why a student was or wasn't engaged. When teaching reflectively, instructors think critically about their methods and look for evidence of effective teaching (Brookfield, 2017). One of the best ways to get real-time feedback on student engagement is to measure it so you can reflect on the results.

Let's say a teacher is having a parent meeting in school. How would it be if the teacher only relied on their perceptions to discuss academic performance? To avoid self-deception and inform you of what interventions may be helpful, the sure way is to measure student engagement using objective tools and resources (Appleton & Silberglitt, 2019)

Measuring student engagement is similar to formative assessment. The essence of formative assessment is to help the student make progress or improve in learning, and to tailor instructional adjustments to the student's individual point of need. Measuring student engagement is important for that same reason. If we measure as we go, we can adjust as needed to improve students' engagement with us and the learning process.

Measuring Student Engagement to Show Students You Care

Sometimes students, especially the partially engaged and disengaged students, are not sure why they are in school or if teachers truly care. It is not unusual to see students exhibit a don't-care attitude, as if to say their lives are not dependent on what a teacher says in the lesson. In addition, some students come to school carrying baggage from family struggles, troubles in their community, and more. Measuring student engagement provides critical information to the teacher for self-reflection and provides tangible evidence that the teacher is concerned and cares about the student and their learning.

Researchers Matthew Kraft and Shaun Dougherty (2013) agree that a student's sense of relatedness to the teacher impacts student engagement. Sometimes this is the only miracle required to turn on a disengaged student. Such a student gets to realize that they are not fighting alone, and that there is a shoulder available to lean on. According to Ross Brenneman (2016), teachers play a critical role in influencing the level of interest and engagement by students, thus igniting students' passion, energy, and investment of time in their quest for knowledge and excellence.

To help show students you care, use the reproducible "Daily Student Engagement Survey" on page 101. Have students complete this survey anonymously as often as you need to help them feel that they have a voice and to assess their engagement. Using this tool daily or weekly allows you to quickly and easily reflect on what minor changes you can make for the next day or next week.

Measuring Student Engagement to Track What Works

Whatever happens within the four walls of the classroom is geared toward facilitating teaching and ultimately learning. While teachers are professionally trained and prepared to implement curriculum and the specific syllabus for every course, there are many variables within the learning environment that may render some pedagogical approaches meaningful or inappropriate. And what works for one student may not work for another. Measuring student engagement can help reveal interesting insights on how students received your well-thought-out lesson.

POWERIDEA

Measuring student engagement reveals interesting insights on how students received your well-thought-out lesson.

For students who repeatedly demonstrate lack of interest whenever a teacher is in class, these data pave the way for the teacher to go back to the drawing board and diagnose their methodology. The teacher may be surprised to realize that the problem was never the student, but rather the approaches used in content delivery. Therefore, a slight change in the delivery may work wonders in subsequent lessons. For example, educator Jane Kise (2021) offers guidance on four key cognitive processing styles and how to effectively distribute unit instruction across all four in her book, *Doable Differentiation: Twelve Strategies to Meet the Needs of All Learners*. She gives the example of a mathematics teacher who changed her strategies to using open and student-centered questions, which helped her learners move from being passive learners to enjoying completing open-ended tasks.

Measuring student engagement requires teachers to avoid rigidly adhering to certain traditions or practices and be willing to adjust as needed. This flexibility becomes a win-win situation for the teacher and the student. It's disheartening for a teacher to see disinterest on students' faces and to imagine what they are losing in the process. Data collected from measuring student engagement will be instrumental in adjusting teaching and assessment methods. For example, knowing what we know about the attention spans of today's students and the benefits of movement and interactive lessons, it would be unfortunate to force students to listen to a lecture style lesson Monday through Thursday and then not understand why students either disconnect or misbehave.

Another example is that some students are better at homework, partly because the home environment is conducive to it. They have quiet spaces to read and to do assignments at home. Other students may not have the space or quiet at home for homework. In this situation, a teacher may inquire about or investigate underlying factors at home that make doing homework difficult.

Owing to external factors, some students may not be very comfortable engaging in activities with students of the opposite gender. Teachers should pay attention to these signals because whatever disinterests a student in class is a recipe for disaster. For example, some disengaged students will convert any excuse into an opportunity to be out of school, including not wanting to be in the company of certain persons during in-class activities. If a teacher sticks to a methodology that a student hates, the student is likely to develop a negative attitude toward the teacher and the subject, causing poor results from one assessment to another. It is imperative for the teacher to drop what does not work and embrace what does work.

Measuring Engagement Criteria

To ensure that you are measuring engagement in a way that is meaningful, use the following three actions: measure, watch, and ask.

1. **Measure daily:** Use the reproducible "Daily Student Engagement Survey" (page 101) to measure engagement. For example, choose a class or a random student to fill out the engagement tool daily.

2. **Watch:** As you deliver your well-prepared lesson, watch the level of engagement from all students. Look at their eyes to see if they are enthusiastically engaged in the conversation and ascertain if it's an engaging conversation about the day's lesson.

3. **Ask:** Finally, after you have measured and watched your students participate in your lesson, ask yourself if you feel that they were engaged. And, if you're not quite sure, ask your students if they felt the lesson was engaging.

When I began as head of school at the Male Leadership Academy, I discovered many students did not perform well in key fourth- and fifth-grade classes, especially behaviorally. It was these grades where I received the most behavior referrals. And because their behavior was not conducive to learning, it affected their performance—or as I theorized, it was the level of engagement that was driving their behavior. While I could have taken the traditional route and depended exclusively on academic scores and behavioral referrals, I wanted to see what was driving, or at least contributing to, the subpar scores and behavior. The three methods that we used were: (1) polling, (2) collaborative engagement, and (3) reflective engagement.

We wanted to get quick data and help students feel they had input. So we decided to simply take a poll. We started polling in October and tied it into the election season. Polling allowed us to check how well students understood the material. We divided the lectures into fifteen-minute chunks, and at the end of each chunk, posted a question for students. In today's environment, you can use tools like Poll Everywhere (www.polleverywhere.com) or the Zoom polling feature (https://zoom.us). Students can answer on their phones or computers. Or you might use a simple fist-to-five approach, asking students to respond to a question by raising a fist to indicate strong disagreement or signal one to five for increasing levels of agreement. Polling allowed us to quickly see how well students understood the material, which prompted my team to reteach portions where the poll showed students' lack of understanding. Our students loved it, my teachers loved it, and relationships soared.

Our second method was collaborative engagement. With this method, we divided students into groups and designated a role for each student within the group. Teachers then assigned the group to work together to complete an assignment. Each person in the group contributed and selected someone from the group to present. We found that even students who did not have high contributions in their small groups increased their learning by listening to their group's peers and then again when their group presented. We then tested individually, and it had a dramatic effect on our scores.

Our third method was reflective engagement, which works best at the end of class. Teachers passed out a reflection sheet asking students what they learned from that day's material. Teachers also created a reflection board to go over the material, and students wrote what they learned from the lesson on the board. Of course, not all students wrote on the board, but everyone read the information and reflected on what they learned. We created reflection sheets so every student could write down what their peers wrote on the board and could study their notes in class or at home.

The biggest tip we learned from these three methods was to keep the students guessing as to how we were going to assess their engagement because, as the old saying goes, familiarity breeds contempt. In other words, we didn't want our engagement measuring process to become so standardized and predictable that our results would become contaminated with student boredom.

As an aside, two of the best survey instruments in the field are Tripod's 7Cs framework of effective teaching survey (www.tripoded.com/surveys) and Check & Connect (https://checkandconnect.umn.edu/research/sei.html), which is a structured intervention that promotes student success and engagement through relationship building and the systematic use of data.

POWERIDEA

Keep the students guessing as to how you are going to assess their engagement because complacency of any form is detrimental to the overall relationship-building and engagement process.

Now that you know all the power moves, we wrap up in the next chapter by moving from creating and measuring engagement to looking at the evidence that engagement has occurred.

Daily Student Engagement Survey

Day of the week: _____ Date: _____

Grade: _____ Subject: _____

Directions: Check the column that matches how you felt about today's lesson.

	Not true	A little true	Mostly true	Very true
Today's class was about something interesting.				
The lesson included information about my culture.				
I was interested or engaged in the lesson.				
Today's class was about something I can use in my culture.				
Today's class was about something that's important to my life right now.				
Today's class was about something I will use.				
Today's class was about something I didn't already know how to do.				

Directions: Check the Yes or No column to indicate how you felt in today's class.

	Yes	No
Happy		
Excited about learning		
Successful		
Smart		
Confused		
Angry		
Proud to be included		
Focused		
Bored		
Did you wish you were doing something different?		
Did you wish you had more chances to share your ideas?		

CHAPTER 10

Understand the Engagement Evidence Chain

> Follow the evidence wherever it leads, and question everything.
> –Neil deGrasse Tyson

In the movie *Jerry Maguire*, Cuba Gooding Jr. plays Rodney "Rod" Tidwell, an all-star professional athlete. Tom Cruise plays Jerry Maguire, Rod's sports agent. In an iconic scene, Rod is fed up with all the back-and-forth with Jerry, so he tells him to "Show me the money." The statement is powerful but simple. For Rod, the money is all the evidence he needs from his agent. When I conduct a cultural audit for school districts, I feel much like Rod. I'm saying, "Show me the evidence!" Show me the evidence that healthy relationships exist between teachers and students that lead to healthy engagement in learning.

The good thing about a classroom coach or those with the coach's mindset is that they want to be part of a winning system. A system whose goals are achievable, measurable, and sustainable. The engagement moves in this book that make up the PowerEngage system are exactly that! However, all systems need assessment, because sometimes it's not the system that fails but the implementation without fidelity to the system's processes.

This chapter explains the engagement evidence chain by beginning with how small links can cause and solve problems along the chain. Then it talks about the different links that make up the engagement evidence change: the expectations link, the exchange link, the executed link, the evaluated link, and the enforced link.

Small Links Make and Fix Big Problems

I will always remember June 15, 1975. My daddy came home with a brand-new bike for me. It was a Schwinn with a banana seat, sport streamers, a horn on the handlebars, and rearview mirrors. It was the Cadillac of bikes in my neighborhood, and all the kids wanted one. Filled with excitement, I ripped off my school clothes, put on my play clothes, grabbed my bike, and rode through the neighborhood like Paul Revere. Unfortunately, twenty minutes into the ride, the chain snapped!

As I returned home, my dad asked, "What happened?" I yelled, "The chain snapped!" He said, "That's OK. We can fix that." We went up to the local hardware store, and he purchased a small chain link to repair the chain system. While repairing it, I realized how important that small link was to the success of my ride and my popularity in the neighborhood. Little did I know then that I was subconsciously learning a valuable lesson that day: regardless of the system's complexity, a small link can cause the entire system to fail. However, finding and fixing the link is all it takes to repair the overall system. This childhood lesson proved to be beneficial in my adulthood.

When I became a school leader in 2015, one of the first things I did was to assess the school culture and its systems of operation. While the culture required a major overhaul, I had a great instructional team, and I discovered that many of the needed systems were in place. However, it was clear that the operational processes (the links) were disconnected, rendering many good systems ineffective. I began to reflect on my childhood lesson on how important a missing link can be to the overall operation of an institution, a corporation, or even a family. I used that experience to follow the evidence chain.

Engagement Evidence Chain Is Vital

A prime example of how important the links are was the Burton Glen Charter Academy project I worked on. The school leader watched the school's average daily attendance number like it was the performance of his favorite stock. He had interventions set up for students once they hit three absences and another set of interventions for when a student hit five. His goal was to do as much as he could to prevent students from achieving the level of *chronic absenteeism*, defined as missing 10 percent or more of school (U.S. Department of Education, 2016a). Chronic absenteeism is different from truancy, which only measures unexcused absences.

A school achieving this magic plateau of 10 percent is akin to students getting on the fast train to low achievement and bad behavior or dropping out altogether (Gershenson, Jacknowitz, & Brannegan, 2017). The school leader also understood that all school systems risk losing valuable funding when daily attendance drops below a specific level. However, while he possessed a system, he did not fully trust the outcomes or data from his system because he was getting too many complaints from parents and teachers refuting the data. Parents said their children were at school on time, while the data said students were not. While the school leader trusted his system, he did not have confidence in its outcomes.

It turns out that both parents and the data were correct. What we found was a missing link in the attendance reporting process. Students arrived at school on time; however, attendance was turned in later in the day. Because the current registrar was just learning the position, they did not enter the data with fidelity. We spoke to parents directly and apologized for the mix-up, tweaked the reporting timing, and provided additional training to the registrar. Measured attendance immediately increased across all grades by 15 percent. Burton Glen Charter Academy ended up winning an award for attendance and engagement from the state.

Taking this lesson to heart as I continued to observe and support schools, I began to build a process to help them quickly find the missing link in their engagement systems. That's when my experience as a school leader and my bike experience became extremely valuable. I built a five-question strategy for assessing school engagement to easily find the missing link.

1. Have I set high, achievable, believable, and desirable engagement expectations for all stakeholders?

2. Have I used the best methods to exchange engagement expectations with stakeholders?

3. Have I executed all engagement strategies with fidelity?

4. Have I evaluated all engagement strategies?

5. Have I enforced engagement expectations with celebration and compassionate accountability?

This five-question system worked so well that I named it the engagement evidence chain. Each link in a chain is important, but the power of a chain is not in the individual links; the power is in the connectivity of its links because that connection makes it possible for the system to work as one. The following chapter sections look at each link.

In addition, to assess the evidence chain, use the reproducible "The Engagement Evidence Chain Assessment" on page 111. This tool is one of my favorites because it helps me to quickly decompress and assess any program or initiative that I am working on. It also allows me to quickly uncover if I or my team have missed an important step in program implementation. Apply this tool to any program or initiative that you are working on.

POWER IDEA

Each link in a chain is important, but the power of a chain is not in the individual links; the power is in the connectivity of its links because that connection makes it possible for the system to work as one.

The Expectations Link

The first link in the engagement evidence chain asks, "Have I set high, achievable, believable, and desirable engagement expectations for all stakeholders?" This question sets the tone and describes the expected outcomes for the school's engagement system. Every subsequent link is measured against the expectations set forth in this link. As you begin to assess your engagement expectations, you're looking for evidence that reasonable and achievable engagement expectations are properly set based on your goals and target audience. For example, let's say your goal is to begin each morning setting the engagement mindset by greeting students with smiles and hugs. Then your first expectation in the link may be for instructional personnel to be in the building by 7:00 a.m. Your next expectation may be that students arrive at a certain time each morning.

If the proper expectations are set, students will be able and motivated to participate and achieve the stated goal. The key when setting expectations is that they must be be achievable, believable, and desirable. To ensure that stakeholder engagement goes beyond the individual and becomes institutional, leaders and staff must create believable, achievable, and desirable engagement expectations for staff, parents, and students. The research on educational leadership tells us, "When the members of a team of educators are confident they have the ability to make a difference in a school, it can have a significant impact on school culture and achievement" (Donohoo, Hattie, & Eells, 2018, p. 41). Achievable and believable means that participants believe that the engagement expectations are possible. Desirable means participants want the outcome expected. The expectations and their benefits are communicated to all stakeholders.

The Exchange Link

The second link in the engagement evidence chain is to ask the question, "Have I used the best methods to *exchange* engagement expectations with stakeholders?"

Journalist William H. Whyte wrote, "The great enemy of communication, we find, is the illusion of it." (Whyte, 1950, p. 174).

Consider our goal of starting each morning by setting an engagement mindset that was mentioned in our expectation link. Here we asked the question, did we *exchange* or communicate that expectation to parents and the entire instructional team? Teachers complain about communication with parents, parents complain about communication with teachers, and schools complain about missed communication with teachers and parents. These complaints show me that their communications link of engagement is broken or missing. All stakeholders believe communication has occurred. They often cite emails, newsletters, or information in the handbook. However, they need to ask themselves, "Is there a sincere desire to have authentic collaborative communication—communication that leads to the achievement of the expectations?"

Lyle Kirtman (2013) offers the following communication advice in his book *Leadership and Teams: The Missing Piece of the Educational Reform Puzzle.*

- Build trust through clear communication and expectations.

- Practice communication that is direct and honest about team commitments and obligation.

- Follow through with actions on all commitments.

- Ensure a clear understanding of written and verbal communication.

- Be comfortable dealing with destructive conflict.

Imagine yourself an American in the middle of the African continent. You are well supplied, but you need to find your way to a U.S. embassy for passage back home. Across Africa, people speak 1,000 to 2,000 different languages, and you have to communicate with someone to get directions to the nearest U.S. embassy (Harvard University, 2023). That's how urgent communication can be to accomplish your goals at school.

Communication must be shared in a language or method that everyone understands. Communication has two parts to it: (1) the sending and (2) the receiving. Merely sending a message does not complete the communication. The message must be received and understood, or it has not been communicated.

The Executed Link

The third link in the engagement evidence chain is to ask the question, "Have I *executed* all engagement expectations with fidelity?" Execution has become a buzzword in sports, in business, and in life, as leaders watch sound strategies fail at the hands of organizations that cannot or will not effectively implement strategies. The following timeless universal truth on program execution says it all:

> Discovering what works does not solve the problem of program effectiveness. Once models and best practices are identified, practitioners are faced with the challenge of implementing programs properly. A poorly implemented program can lead to failure as easily as a poorly designed one. (Mihalic, Irwin, Fagan, Ballard, & Elliot, 2004, p. 2.)

There is always a healthy tension between planning and execution. At the planning table, everyone has ideas and a vision, and most often, the participants are excited about the new project. However, once the expected goal to achieve high engagement has been decided, the plan to achieve high stakeholder engagement must be executed.

Each stakeholder is responsible for doing their part to achieve engagement. Each stakeholder must do their part to honor the relationship. Leadership must maintain the course of the vision. Staff must have the will and skill to deliver rigorous content in multiple ways to all students. Students must take greater responsibility for their learning, and parents must be willing to support, partner, and monitor academic progress.

When these key stakeholders don't bring their execution A game consistently, clearly, and in multiple forms to achieve high levels of engagement, then an important link in the evidence engagement chain is already broken. And when the chain is broken, the outcomes will not be predictable, reliable, or scalable.

The Evaluated Link

The fourth link in the engagement evidence chain asks the question, "Have I *evaluated* all engagement strategies?" A U.S. Department of Education (2016b) report states that "Using, generating, and sharing evidence about effective strategies to support students gives stakeholders an important tool to accelerate student learning" (p. 2).

Evaluating your efforts to build healthy relationships so that students engage does two things: (1) it confirms that you have implemented your strategies with fidelity, and (2) it provides you and others the quantifiable evidence that what you're doing is working so that you can share it and duplicate it. I like the way U.S. President Ronald Reagan phrased it when he was preparing for talks with Mikhail Gorbachev in 1986: "Trust, but verify" (Swaim, 2016).

As an example, when purchasing a new program for my school or evaluating relationship and engagement initiatives for one of my school engagement audits, I have learned to ask the following questions.

1. How is it being rolled out?

2. Will the rollout likely lead to meeting the outcomes set by the program?

3. If we have a program in which there are fifteen sessions, are all the sessions being delivered?

4. Are sessions being delivered as written?

5. Are sessions being delivered in the time sequence that was recommended?

6. Were the people delivering the program trained well enough to succeed?

Only when this link is done correctly can you proceed to the next link and have compassionate, informed conversations while providing support. When the evaluation link is broken, your program or initiative will be hard to critique or celebrate.

The Enforced Link

The fifth and final link in the engagement evidence chain asks two important questions: "Have I *enforced* engagement expectations with celebration and compassionate accountability?" "Have I provided support when things are not working?"

POWERIDEA

"Have I *enforced* engagement expectations with celebration and compassionate accountability?" "Have I provided support when things are not working?"

To start, let's clear up some possible confusion between two words: *accountable* and *responsible*. Whatever the dictionary says, we all know what accountable means in our schools. The person who is accountable is the person who gets the credit when everything succeeds or takes the blame if it fails. *Accountable* means you are the source of the program, and you are the ultimate authority. I learned from being a building leader that what's really important is that only one person can be accountable for something. On the flip side, *responsible* means you have ownership over implementation or getting tasks done around that initiative.

Generally, only one person is accountable, but multiple people can be responsible, and sometimes you can be both accountable and responsible. So, think of it as wearing two different hats, but it's important to differentiate between the two hats.

Let me give you an example. Each morning at my school, students arrived at 7:40 a.m. My transportation director was responsible for organizing bus routes and managing his team's four pickups and drop-offs. He was accountable each day for the smooth and safe pickup and arrival of all students; however, his team of drivers was responsible for carrying out the task. If there was ever an issue with a student not picked up or dropped off at the wrong stop, he was held accountable; however, his drivers were responsible. All stakeholders and students shared one expectation, which was that students would be picked up and delivered to the school and transported home safely.

In the rare times when this expectation wasn't met, there were compassionate consequences as defined in Classroom Coaches Provide Compassionate Consequences (page 37 in chapter 3). Additionally, at the end of each semester, we celebrated the success of our transportation system by honoring the director and his team.

Another example is our parent engagement system. To increase parent engagement, we implemented a Parent University using strategies detailed in chapter 7 (page 69). What made the program unique is that it created conversation and a connection between teachers and parents around academics. However, the program did not do as well as we hoped, and we had invested a huge part of our title funding into it. As the person accountable for its success, I looked at those responsible for its implementation. What I found was that the program was not implemented with fidelity, so the results were skewed. To get a more accurate assessment, I had to reinforce the importance of the program by supporting some of my instructional team with more research and by celebrating others who had success with the program.

What became very clear was when the process or people most responsible for achieving high engagement are not celebrated or willing to be corrected, then an important link in the evidence chain is once again broken. However, when you see all five links working in the evidence chain, you will know you are on your way to building great relationships, and that high levels of engagement are possible, probable, and present.

To help you on your way, you can use the "Chart of Power Moves" on page 113 that includes all the moves we've discussed.

The Engagement Evidence Chain Assessment

Directions: Each evidence link is important for evaluating your process. Any link missing important steps or that is incomplete factors into the success of your program. Identify evidence that the program link is completed. Add additional feedback if there are important need-to-do steps for your success. *Important: Any weak or broken link requires attention to ensure the success of your program.*

School: _____ Date: _____

Engagement Task or Program Being Evaluated: _____

Evaluators: _____

Evidence Links	Evidence (Evidence that link is completed or accurate.)	Steps (Steps needed to strengthen a link.)
Expectations of Program 1. Our program expectations have been clearly defined. 2. Our program outcomes have been clearly defined. 3. There is initial belief and support that the program can meet our needs.		
Embraced 1. We have a program champion who consistently helps and inspires others about the benefits of this program. 2. Our building administrator supports the program.		
Exchanged 1. Our program expectations have been communicated to each stakeholder in their language and in a timely manner. 2. Our program procedures have been documented and shared with all stakeholders. 3. Our stakeholders have been trained and understand the program benefits and features.		

continued ▶

Evidence Links	Evidence (Evidence that link is completed or accurate.)	Steps (Steps needed to strengthen a link.)
Executed 1. Teachers executed the important program steps with sincerity and fidelity. 2. Parents executed the important program steps with sincerity and fidelity. 3. Students executed the important program steps with sincerity and fidelity.		
Evaluated 1. We evaluated the execution of the program in a timely manner. 2. We evaluated the execution of the program for each stakeholder. 3. We shared the data with key stakeholders. 4. We made tweaks to the program based on the data and our unique needs.		
Enforced 1. We have a system of compassionate support for struggling stakeholders. 2. We have a system of compassionate accountability for stakeholders who do not follow program procedures.		
More Tasks to Ensure Success 1. _____ 2. _____ 3. _____		

Chart of Power Moves

Directions: Choose any power move at any given time with any given student or group of students. You can use more than one at a time if it works for you. Power moves are not chronological, sequential, or scaffolded. This table includes a few suggestions on when to implement each one.

Power Moves	Best Time to Use This Power Move
Adopt the classroom coach mindset. (Chapter 3)	If you are a new teacher (five years or fewer), use this as the foundational strategy to give you the mindset needed to build relationships with all three groups of students: the engaged, the partially engaged, and the disengaged. If you are an experienced teacher, use this strategy to gain a new perspective.
Know your why for teaching. (Chapter 4)	Teaching is a journey, and we can often lose our way. In those moments when you question your decision to teach, this power move reminds you of your purpose and the importance of what you do for students.
Help students find their *high why*. (Chapter 5)	For many students, learning is abstract. This power move provides students with educational context and lets them know that they mean more to you than just board work, homework, tests, and grades. It lets them know you care about preparing them for whatever life brings their way.
Foster cooperative competition. (Chapter 6)	We all lack motivation from time to time and one of the best ways to introduce excitement and motivation is through competition. Using this strategy couples the benefits of competition with the benefits of cooperation.
Educate and celebrate parents as partners. (Chapter 7)	Teaching students without the support of their families is a heavy load to lift. Use this power move when parents have gotten too comfortable or are not sure how to engage around academics.
Target your boys. (Chapter 8)	Use this strategy if you recognize or suspect that there are unconscious biases in your classroom or school. Also use this strategy if boys have not found their place academically in your classroom or school.
Measure student engagement frequently. (Chapter 9)	This strategy is best used on a weekly basis to get feedback from your students. Your tests tell you what they don't understand; this power move helps you understand why they may not be performing. Or use this power move simply to give students the feeling that their input matters.

Epilogue

Since the early 2000s, I have had the pleasure and blessing of traveling and training instructional teams all over the United States and other countries. The one thing that is consistent and predictable in every classroom, culture, and country is that teachers don't go into this profession chasing compensation: it's a calling! One doesn't decide to educate urban students, underserved students, disabled students, or English learners to chase personal titles or accomplishments.

Educating the world's students boils down to having a passion to fulfill one's purpose. There is something deep down inside that screams in a way that can't be ignored, "I want to help turn on the learning light bulb for students!"

Knowing and understanding that fact makes my heart go out to my fellow educators. So I set out on this journey to provide strategies that many educators don't get while in college or even in their school. These proven strategies didn't require building approval or district funding. Classroom coaches could implement these strategies tomorrow. Power Engage gives you just that!

Therefore, now that you're highly qualified and certified, my dream for you is to add the mindset of a classroom coach to your classroom teaching, add the strategy and benefits of building and nurturing performance-based relationships to your mindset, and then sit back and watch the engagement dominoes fall.

References and Resources

American Sociological Association. (2016). *Early behavior problems impact educational attainment of boys more than girls.* Accessed at www.asanet.org/news_item/early-behavior -problems-impact-educational-attainment-boys-more-girls on June 16, 2023.

Appleton, J. J., & Silberglitt, B. (2019). Chapter 22—Student engagement instrument as a tool to support the link between assessment and intervention: A comparison of implementations in two districts. In J. A. Fredricks, A.L. Reschly, & S. L. Christenson (Eds.), *Handbook of Student Engagement Interventions* (pp. 325–343). Cambridge, MA: Academic Press. https://doi.org/10.1016/B978-0-12-813413-9.00022-X

Babey, S. H., Wolstein, J., Becker, T. L., & Scheitler, A. J. (2019, September). *School discipline practices associated with adolescent school connectedness and engagement.* Los Angeles: UCLA Center for Health Policy Research. Accessed at http://resource.nlm.nih.gov/101757870 on March 23, 2023.

Beattie, H., Rich, M., & Evans, P. (2015). *The case for the missing R.* Alexandria, VA: ASCD. Accessed at https://upforlearning.org/wp-content/uploads/2021/04/CaseOfTheMissingR -Ed-Leadership-Final.pdf on March 24, 2023.

Berger, N., & Fisher, P. (2013, August 22). *A well-educated workforce is key to state prosperity.* Economic Policy Institute. Accessed at https://bit.ly/3HQK673 on July 7, 2022.

Binu, P. M. (2020). The role of feedback in classroom instruction. *Journal of ELTIF, 5*(4), 7–11. Accessed at www.researchgate.net/publication/341001451_The_role_of_feedback_in _classroom_instruction on July 11, 2022.

Blackwell, L. S., Trzesniewski, K. H., & Dweck, C. S. (2007). Implicit theories of intelligence predict achievement across an adolescent transition: A longitudinal study and an intervention. *Child Development, 78*(1), 246–263.

Blazer, C., & Gonzalez Hernandez, V. (2018). *Student dropout: Risk factors, impact of prevention programs, and effective strategies.* Miami, FL: Research Services. Accessed at https://files.eric.ed .gov/fulltext/ED587683.pdf on March 24, 2023.

Brandenburger, A., & Nalebuff, B. (2021, January). The rules of co-opetition. *Harvard Business Review.* Accessed at https://hbr.org/2021/01/the-rules-of-co-opetition on June 16, 2023.

Brenneman, R. (2016, March 22). Gallup student poll finds engagement in school dropping by grade level. *Education Week*. Accessed at www.edweek.org/leadership/gallup-student-poll -finds-engagement-in-school-dropping-by-grade-level/2016/03 on March 22, 2016.

Brookfield, S. D. (2017). *Becoming a critically reflective teacher* (2nd ed.). San Francisco: Jossey Bass.

Brooks, C., DeJong, S., Lytton, K., Pacheco, R., & Pradhan, S. (2020, November 9). *Chronic absenteeism: A research review*. Northampton, MA: Collaborative for Educational Services. Accessed at www.hfpg.org/application/files/7416/1946/4633/Chronic_Absenteeism _Research_Review_for_website.pdf on July 30, 2022.

Burnette, J. L., O'Boyle, E. H., VanEpps, E. M., Pollack, J. M., & Finkel, E. J. (2013). Mind-sets matter: A meta-analytic review of implicit theories and self-regulation. *Psychological Bulletin, 139*(3), 655–701.

Carrera, C. (2022, June 30). Newark's 2022 Teacher of the Year says kids strive when they feel accepted. *Chalkbeat Newark*. Accessed at https://newark.chalkbeat.org/2022/6/30 /23188034/newark-science-teacher-year-2022-jessica-tavares-acceptance on July 7, 2022.

Center for Performance Improvement. (2017, June 14). How can YOU hit a target you do not even have? *Medium*. Accessed at https://medium.centerforperformanceimprovement.com /goals-how-can-you-hit-a-target-you-do-not-even-have-793b93e2962 on March 24, 2023.

Center for Popular Democracy & Urban Youth Collaborative. (2017, April). *The $746 million a year school-to-prison pipeline: The ineffective, discriminatory, and costly process of criminalizing New York City students*. New York: Author. Accessed at https://populardemocracy.org/sites /default/files/Executive%20Summary.pdf on January 19, 2023.

Chen, I. (2014, August 18). How a bigger purpose can motivate students to learn. *KQED*. Accessed at www.kqed.org/mindshift/37020/how-a-bigger-purpose-can-motivate-students -to-learn on January 1, 2022.

Chetty, R., Friedman, J. N., & Rockoff, J. E. (2014). Measuring the impacts of teachers II: Teacher value-added and student outcomes in adulthood. *American Economic Review, 104*(9), 2633–2679. Accessed at https://pubs.aeaweb.org/doi/pdfplus/10.1257/aer.104.9.2633 on March 24, 2023.

Christenson, S. L., Reschly, A. L., & Wylie, C. (Eds.). (2012). *Handbook of research on student engagement*. New York: Springer. Accessed at https://doi.org/10.1007/978-1-4614-2018-7 on July 11, 2022.

Cleveland Clinic. (2021, January 28). *Stress*. Accessed at https://my.clevelandclinic.org/health /articles/11874-stress on June 27, 2023.

Competition (n.d.). In *Wikipedia*. Accessed at https://en.wikipedia.org/wiki/Competition#cite _note-1 on March 27, 2023.

Cooper, K. S. (2014). Eliciting engagement in the classroom: A mixed-methods examination of teaching practices. *American Educational Research Journal, 51*(2), 363–402. Accessed at www.knoxeducation.com/sites/main/files/file-attachments/2_engagement.pdf?1487366119 on July 7, 2022.

Corak, M. (2017, September). *'Inequality is the root of social evil,' or maybe not? Two stories about inequality and public policy*. [Discussion paper no. 11005]. Bonn, Germany: IZA Institute of Labor Economics. Accessed at https://docs.iza.org/dp11005.pdf on March 14, 2023.

De Kraker-Pauw, E., Van Wesel, F., Krabbendam, L., & Van Atteveldt, N. (2017). Teacher mindsets concerning the malleability of intelligence and the appraisal of achievement in the context of feedback. *Frontiers in Psychology, 8.* https://doi.org/10.3389/fpsyg.2017.01594

Diliberti, M. K., Schwartz, H. L., & Grant, D. (2021). *Stress topped the reasons why public school teachers quit, even before COVID-19.* Santa Monica, CA: RAND Corporation. Accessed at www.rand.org/pubs/research_reports/RRA1121-2.html on March 24, 2023.

Donohoo, J., Hattie, J., & Eells, R. (2018). The power of collective efficacy. *Educational Leadership, 75*(6), 40–44. Accessed at www.ascd.org/el/articles/the-power-of-collective -efficacy on July 5, 2023.

Duckworth, A. (2016). *Grit: the power of passion and perseverance.* New York: Scribner.

DuFour, R., DuFour, R., Eaker, R., & Many, T. (2010). *Learning by doing: A handbook for professional learning communities at work* (2nd ed.). Bloomington, IN: Solution Tree Press.

DuFour, R., DuFour, R., Eaker, R., Many, T. W., & Mattos, M. (2016). *Learning by doing: A handbook for Professional Learning Communities at Work* (3rd ed.). Bloomington, IN: Solution Tree Press.

DuFour, R., & Eaker, R. (1998). *Professional Learning Communities at Work: Best practices for enhancing student achievement.* Bloomington, IN: Solution Tree Press.

Dweck, C. S. (2016). *Mindset: The new psychology of success.* New York: Random House.

Edthena. (2024). *Think you know what culturally responsive teaching is? you might not.* [Blog post]. Accessed at www.edthena.com/what-is-culturally-responsive-teaching on June 27, 2023.

Encyclopedia.com. (n.d.) *Archimedes and the simple machines that moved the world.* Accessed at www.encyclopedia.com/science/encyclopedias-almanacs-transcripts-and-maps/archimedes -and-simple-machines-moved-world on July 24, 2023.

Fink, J. L. W. (2017, June 20). *How movement helps boys learn.* Accessed at www.understanding boys.com.au/how-movement-helps-boys-learn on June 20, 2023.

Ferguson, R. F., & Danielson, C. (2014). How framework for teaching and Tripod 7Cs evidence distinguish key components of effective teaching. In T. J. Kane, K. A. Kerr, & R. C. Pianta (Eds.), *Designing teacher evaluation systems: New guidance from the measures of effective teaching project* (pp. 98–143). San Francisco: Jossey-Bass. https://doi.org/10.1002/97811 19210856.ch4

Ferguson, R. (2015). *The influence of teaching beyond standardized test scores: Engagement, mindsets, and agency.* The Achievement Gap Initiative at Harvard University. Accessed at www.aitsl.edu.au/docs/default-source/general/the-influence-of-teaching-(2015).pdf on July 7, 2022.

Forster, D. E., Pedersen, E. J., Smith, A., McCullough, M. E., & Lieberman, D. (2017). Benefit valuation predicts gratitude. *Evolution and Human Behavior, 38,* 18–26. Accessed at https://pages.ucsd.edu/~memccullough/Papers/2017-BenefitValuationPredictsGratitude.pdf on June 20, 2023.

Froiland, J. M. (2013). Parent educational expectations. In J. Ainsworth (Ed.), *Sociology of education: An A–Z guide* (pp. 569–570). Thousand Oaks, CA: SAGE. Accessed at www.research gate.net/publication/287206227_Parent_educational_expectations on July 27, 2022.

Gaille, L. (2017, December 1) *16 Pros and Cons of Title IX.* [Blog post]. Accessed at https://vittana.org/16-pros-and-cons-of-title-ix on June 16, 2023.

Games and Learning. (2014, August 11). *Research: Competitive games can drive student engagement.* Accessed at www.gamesandlearning.org/2014/08/11/research-competitive -games-can-drive-student-engagement/ on June 19, 2023.

Gartmeier, M., Gebhardt, M., & Dotger, B. (2016). How do teachers evaluate their parent communication competence? Latent profiles and relationships to workplace behaviors. *Teaching and Teacher Education, 55,* 207–216. https://doi.org/10.1016/j.tate.2016.01.009

Gershenson, S., Jacknowitz, A., & Brannegan, A. (2017). Are student absences worth the worry in U.S. primary schools? *Education Finance and Policy, 12*(2), 137–165.

Gladwell, M. (2002). *The tipping point: How little things can make a big difference.* Boston: Back Bay Books.

Goegan, L. D., & Daniels, L. M. (2022). Just a little healthy competition: Teacher perceptions of competition and social comparison in the classroom. *Canadian Journal of School Psychology, 37*(4), 394–405.

Hammond, Z. (2015). *Culturally responsive teaching and the brain: Promoting authentic engagement and rigor among culturally and linguistically diverse students.* Thousand Oaks, CA: Corwin Press.

Harvard University. (2023). *Introduction to African languages.* Accessed at https://alp.fas .harvard.edu/introduction-african-languages on June 19, 2023.

Hattie, J. (2009). *Visible learning: A synthesis of over 800 meta-analyses relating to achievement.* New York: Routledge.

Hattie, J. A. C., & Yates, G. C. R. (2014). Using feedback to promote learning. In V. A. Benassi, C. E. Overson, & C. M. Hakala (Eds.), *Applying science of learning in education: Infusing psychological science into the curriculum* (pp. 45–58). Washington, DC: American Psychological Association.

Henderson, A. T., & Mapp, K. L. (2002). *A new wave of evidence: The impact of school, family, and community connections on student achievement.* Austin, TX: Southwest Educational Development Laboratory. Accessed at https://sedl.org/connections/resources/evidence.pdf on March 27, 2023.

Herrnstein, R. J., & Murray, C. (1994). *The bell curve: Intelligence and class structure in American life.* New York: Free Press.

Hirshkowitz, M., Whiton, K., Albert, S. M., Alessi, C., Bruni, O., et al. (2015). National Sleep Foundation's updated sleep duration recommendations: final report. *Sleep health, 1*(4), 233–243. https://doi.org/10.1016/j.sleh.2015.10.004

Howard, M. (2015, July 15). More than one valedictorian? That's a real winner of a problem. *Time.* Accessed at https://time.com/3958000/more-than-one-valedictorian-thats-a-real -winner-of-a-problem on June 16, 2023.

Ingersoll, R. M., Merrill, E., Stuckey, D., & Collins, G. (2018). *Seven trends: the transformation of the teaching force.* Philadelphia, PA: CPRE Research Reports. Accessed at https://repository .upenn.edu/server/api/core/bitstreams/eaeb5e1f-e7be-4843-8f0f-ea20b9fda13e/content on July 6, 2023.

Image of Success. (n.d.). *The I.M.A.G.E. culture transformation system.* Accessed at www.power parentingu.com on May 22, 2023.

Johnson, D. W., Johnson, R. T., & Smith, K. A. (2014). Cooperative learning: Improving university instruction by basing practice on validated theory. *Journal on Excellence in College Teaching, 25*(3&4), 85–118. Accessed at http://static.pseupdate.mior.ca.s3.amazonaws.com /media/links/Cooperative_learn_validated_theory.pdf on June 19, 2022.

Kanold, T. (2017). *HEART! Fully forming your professional life as a teacher and leader.* Bloomington, IN: Solution Tree Press.

Keller, G., & Papasan, J. (2013). *The ONE thing: The surprisingly simple truth behind extraordinary results.* Portland, OR: Bard Press.

Kim, E. S., Kawachi, I., Chen, Y., & Kubzansky, L. D. (2017). Association between purpose in life and objective measures of physical function in older adults. *JAMA Psychiatry, 74*(10), 1039–1045. https://doi.org/10.1001/jamapsychiatry.2017.2145

Kirtman, L. (2013). *Leadership and teams: The missing piece of the educational reform puzzle.* New York: Pearson.

Kise, J. A. G. (2021). *Doable differentiation: Twelve strategies to meet the needs of all learners.* Bloomington, IN: Solution Tree Press.

Kraft, M. A., & Dougherty, S. M. (2013). The effect of teacher-family communication on student engagement: Evidence from a randomized field experiment. *Journal of Research on Educational Effectiveness, 6*(3), 199–222. Accessed at https://scholar.harvard.edu/mkraft /publications/effect-teacher-family-communication-student-engagement-evidence -randomized-field on March 27, 2023.

Li, C., Cao, J., & Li, T. M. H. (2016). Eustress or distress: An empirical study of perceived stress in everyday college life (pp. 1209–1217). *Proceedings of the 2016 ACM International Joint Conference on Pervasive and Ubiquitous Computing.* Heidelberg, Germany: Association for Computing Machinery. http://dx.doi.org/10.1145/2968219.2968309

Longfellow, H. W. (1860). *Paul Revere's Ride.* Accessed at https://poets.org/poem/paul-reveres -ride on July 11, 2023.

Losen, D. J., & Whitaker, A. (n.d.). *11 million days lost: Race, discipline, and safety at U.S. public schools* (Part 1). Center for Civil Rights Remedies & American Civil Liberties Union of Southern California. Accessed at www.aclu.org/sites/default/files/field_document/final_11 -million-days_ucla_aclu.pdf on March 24, 2023.

Mahbubani, R., & Ma, A. (2020, March 10). Italy enters its first day of a nationwide coronavirus lockdown as it becomes the worst-hit country outside China. *Business Insider.* Accessed at www.businessinsider.com/italy-prime-minister-extends-coronavirus-restriction -zone-entire-country-2020-3 on June 16, 2023.

Mapp, K. L., & Kuttner, P. J. (2013). *Partners in education: A dual capacity-building framework for family-school partnerships.* Arlington, VA: SEDL.

Marzano Center. (2017). *The Marzano teacher evaluation model and the Marzano focused teacher evaluation model.* Blairsville, PA: Learning Sciences International. Accessed at www.marzano center.com/wp-content/uploads/sites/4/2019/04/FTEM_Updated_Michigan_08312017.pdf on March 27, 2023.

Marzano, R. J.(2003). *Classroom management that works: Research-based strategies for every teacher*. Alexandria, VA: ASCD.

Marzano, R. J. (2012). *Marzano levels of school effectiveness*. Accessed at www.wyoleg.gov /interimcommittee/2012/z02marzanolevels.pdf on June 16, 2023.

Mason, B. A., Hajovsky, D. B., McCune, L. A., & Turek, J. J. (2017). Conflict, closeness, and academic skills: A longitudinal examination of the teacher-student relationship. *School Psychology Review, 46*(2), 177–189. https://doi.org/10.17105/SPR-2017-0020.V46-2

Maslow, A. H. (1943). A theory of human motivation. *Psychological Review,* 50(4), 370–396.

Massachusetts Department of Education. (n.d.). *Culturally responsive and sustaining schools and classrooms*. Accessed at www.doe.mass.edu/rlo/instruction/culturally-resp-sust/index.html on March 24, 2023.

Mattos, M. (2017). *Timebomb: the cost of dropping out* [DVD]. Bloomington, IN: Solution Tree Press.

McCold, P., & Wachtel, T. (2003, August 10–15). *In pursuit of paradigm: A theory of restorative justice* [Conference presentation]. XIII World Congress of Criminology, Rio de Janeiro, Brazil. Accessed at www.iirp.edu/images/pdf/paradigm.pdf on March 27, 2023.

Mihalic, S., Irwin, K., Fagan, A., Ballard, D., & Elliott, D. (2004). *Successful program implementation: Lessons from blueprints*. Washington, DC: U.S. Department of Justice Office of Justice Programs. Accessed at www.ojp.gov/pdffiles1/ojjdp/204273.pdf on March 27, 2023.

Mindset. (n.d.). In *The Free Dictionary by Farlex*. Accessed at https://medical-dictionary. thefreedictionary.com/mindset on July 10, 2022.

Morris, S. (2009, October 4). *Domino chain reaction (geometric growth in action)* [Video file]. Accessed at https://youtu.be/y97rBdSYbkg on July 7, 2022.

Muhammad, A. (2018). *Transforming school culture: How to overcome staff division*. Bloomington, IN: Solution Tree Press.

National Center for Education Statistics. (n.d.). *Fast facts: Back-to-school statistics*. Accessed at https://bit.ly/3nJ7GvC on July 5, 2022.

National Center for Education Statistics. (2017). Table 318.10: Degrees conferred by postsecondary institutions, by level of degree and sex of student: Selected years, 1869–70 through 2027–28. *Digest of Education Statistics*. Accessed at https://nces.ed.gov/programs /digest/d17/tables/dt17_318.10.asp on December 15, 2022.

National Center for Education Statistics. (2019a). Table 221.20: Percentage of students at or above selected National Assessment of Educational Progress (NAEP) reading achievement levels, by grade and selected student characteristics: Selected years, 2005 through 2019. *Digest of Education Statistics*. Accessed at https://nces.ed.gov/programs/digest/d19/tables /dt19_221.20.asp on March 27, 2023.

National Center for Education Statistics. (2019b). Table 222.10: Average National Assessment of Educational Progress (NAEP) mathematics scale score, by sex, race/ethnicity, and grade: Selected years, 1990 through 2019. *Digest of Education Statistics*. Accessed at https://nces .ed.gov/programs/digest/d19/tables/dt19_222.10.asp on March 27, 2023.

National Center for Education Statistics. (2020). Table 318.10: Degrees conferred by postsecondary institutions, by level of degree and sex of student: Selected years, 1869-70 through 2029-30. *Digest of Educational Statistics.* Accessed at https://nces.ed.gov/programs /digest/d20/tables/dt20_318.10.asp on June 16, 2023.

Neilson, G. L., & Pasternack, B. A. (2005). *Results: Keep what's good, fix what's wrong, and unlock great performance.* New York: Crown Business.

Northwestern University Feinberg School of Medicine. (2012, June 5). *Changing one bad habit has domino effect.* Accessed at https://news.feinberg.northwestern.edu/2012/06/05/domino _effect on July 7, 2022.

Oberle, E., & Schonert-Reichl, K. A. (2016). Stress contagion in the classroom? The link between classroom teacher burnout and morning cortisol in elementary school students. *Social Science & Medicine, 159,* 30–37. https://doi.org/10.1016/j.socscimed.2016.04.031

Olson, A., & Peterson, R. L. (2015, April). *Strategy brief: Student engagement.* Lincoln, NE: University of Nebraska-Lincoln and the Nebraska Department of Education. Accessed at https://k12engagement.unl.edu/strategy-briefs/Student%20Engagement%2011-10 -15%20.pdf on March 27, 2023.

Olympics YouTube Channel. (2021, May 1). *The ultimate display of determination! Ft. John Akhwari* [Video file]. Accessed at www.youtube.com/watch?v=tNC2r4MOb1w on June 27, 2023.

Owens, J. (2016). Early childhood behavior problems and the gender gap in educational attainment in the United States. *Sociology of Education, 89*(3), 236–258. Accessed at https://watson.brown.edu/files/watson/imce/news/explore/2016/SOE_July_2016_Jayanti _Owens_Study.pdf on March 15, 2022.

Poklar, A. E. (2018). *Urban teacher-student relationship quality, teacher burnout, and cultural competence* [Doctoral dissertation, Cleveland State University]. OhioLINK Electronic Theses and Dissertations Center. Accessed at http://rave.ohiolink.edu/etdc/view?acc_num=csu15 44051173124532 on June 19,2023.

Park, S., & Holloway, S. D. (2013). No parent left behind: predicting parental involvement in adolescents' education within a sociodemographically diverse population. *The Journal of Educational Research, 106*(2):105–119 www.tandfonline.com/doi/abs/10.1080/00220 671.2012.667012

Pew Research Center. (2016, October 6). *The state of American jobs.* Accessed at www.pewresearch.org/social-trends/2016/10/06/1-changes-in-the-american-workplace on July 11, 2022.

Police Executive Research Forum. (2019, September). *The workforce crisis, and what police agencies are doing about it.* Washington, DC: Author. Accessed at www.policeforum.org /assets/WorkforceCrisis.pdf on March 27, 2023.

Popoff, E. (n.d.). *Learning with a purpose: Preparing today's students to navigate an increasingly ambiguous future.* Washington, DC: Whiteboard Advisors. Accessed at https://fs.hub spotusercontent00.net/hubfs/4906503/Offers/Learning%20with%20a%20Purpose_ v.FINAL3.9.pdf on June 15, 2022.

Prochnow, K. (2018, February 17). *Academic competitions help student's* [sic] *gain the soft-skills needed for success.* Accessed at https://bit.ly/3HPqVuj on January 5, 2020.

Protopsaltis, S., & Baum, S. (2019, January). *Does online education live up to its promise? A look at the evidence and implications for federal policy.* Accessed at https://jesperbalslev.dk/wp-content/uploads/2020/09/OnlineEd.pdf on July 11, 2022.

Reardon, S. F., Fahle, E. M., Kalogrides, D., Podolsky, A., & Zárate, R. C. (2019). Gender achievement gaps in U.S. school districts. *American Educational Research Journal, 56*(6), 2474–2508. https://doi.org/10.3102/0002831219843824

Reece, A., Kellerman, G., & Robichaux, A. (2017). *Meaning and purpose at work.* San Francisco, CA: BetterUp. Accessed at https://f.hubspotusercontent40.net/hubfs/9253440/Asset%20PDFs/Promotions_Assets_Whitepapers/BetterUp-Meaning%26Purpose.pdf on June 16, 2023.

Reeves, R. V., Buckner, E., & Smith E. (2021, January 12). The unreported gender gap in high school graduation rates. *Brookings.* Accessed at www.brookings.edu/blog/up-front/2021/01/12/the-unreported-gender-gap-in-high-school-graduation-rates on May 4, 2023.

Reeves, R. V. & Nzau, S. (2021). Poverty hurts the boys the most: Inequality at the intersection of class and gender. *Brookings.* Accessed at www.brookings.edu/research/poverty-hurts-the-boys-the-most-inequality-at-the-intersection-of-class-and-gender on June 16, 2023.

Reeves, R. V. (2022). *Of boys and men: Why the modern male is struggling, why it matters, and what to do about it.* Washington, D.C.: Brookings Institution Press.

Relationship. (2015). In *New Oxford American Dictionary, third edition.* Accessed at https://bit.ly/3O3RVs8 on July 24, 2023.

Rosenthal, R., & Jacobson, L. (1968). *Pygmalion in the classroom: Teacher expectation and pupils' intellectual development.* New York: Holt, Rinehart and Winston.

The School District of Philadelphia. (2021, October 1). *Family involvement vs. family engagement: What's the difference?* Accessed at www.philasd.org/face/2021/10/01/family-involvement-vs-family-engagement-whats-the-difference on July 15, 2022.

Serrat, O. (2017). Asking effective questions. In *Knowledge solutions: Tools, methods, and approaches to drive organizational performance.* Singapore: Springer.

Sigman, M. (2012, April 18). *When everyone gets a trophy, no one wins* [Blog post]. Huffpost. Accessed at www.huffpost.com/entry/when-everyone-gets-a-trop_b_1431319 on March 27, 2023.

Skiba, R. J. (2014). The failure of zero tolerance. *Reclaiming Children and Youth, 22*(4), 27–33. Accessed at https://reclaimingjournal.com/sites/default/files/journal-article-pdfs/22_4_Skiba.pdf on March 27, 2023.

Suor, J. H., Sturge-Apple, M. L., Davies, P. T., Cicchetti, D., & Manning, L. G. (2015). Tracing differential pathways of risk: Associations among family adversity, cortisol, and cognitive functioning in childhood. *Child Development, 86*(4), 1142–1158. https://doi.org/10.1111/cdev.12376

Statistics Canada. (2021, October 14). *Elementary-secondary education survey, 2019/2020.* Accessed at www150.statcan.gc.ca/n1/daily-quotidien/211014/dq211014c-eng.htm on July 5, 2022.

Stress. (n.d.) In *National Cancer Institute's online dictionary.* Accessed at www.cancer.gov /publications/dictionaries/cancer-terms/def/stress on March 24, 2023.

Swaim, B. (2016, March 11). 'Trust, but verify': An untrustworthy political phrase. *The Washington Post.* Accessed at www.washingtonpost.com/opinions/trust-but-verify-an -untrustworthy-political-phrase/2016/03/11/da32fb08-db3b-11e5-891a-4ed04f4213e8 _story.html on January 17, 2023.

Szabo, S., Yoshida, M., Filakovszky, J., & Juhasz, G. (2017). "Stress" is 80 years old: From Hans Selye original paper in 1936 to recent advances in GI ulceration. *Current Pharmaceutical Design, 23*(27), 4029–4041. https://doi.org/10.2174/1381612823666170622110046

Terkel, S. (1974). *Working: People talk about what they do all day and how they feel about what they do.* New York: Pantheon Books.

University of Michigan Department of History. (n.d.). *Deconstructing the model minority at the University of Michigan.* Accessed at https://aapi.umhistorylabs.lsa.umich.edu/s/aapi _michigan/page/education On June 22, 2023.

U.S. Department of Education. (2004, April 23). *Parental involvement: Title I, part A.* Washington, DC: Author. Accessed at https://ed.sc.gov/sites/scdoe/assets/File/programs -services/79/documents/ParentInolvementNon-RegulatoryGuidance.pdf on July 8, 2022.

U.S. Department of Education. (2016a). *Chronic absenteeism in the nation's schools: A hidden educational crisis.* Accessed at www2.ed.gov/datastory/chronicabsenteeism.html on June 19, 2023.

U.S. Department of Education. (2016b). *Non-regulatory guidance: Using evidence to strengthen education investments.* Washington, DC: Author. Accessed at https://region7comprehensive center.org/wp-content/uploads/securepdfs/2020/07/01-guidanceuseseinvestment.pdf on March 27, 2023.

U.S. Government Accountability Office. (2018, March). *K–12 education: Discipline disparities for Black students, boys, and students with disabilities.* Washington, DC: Author. Accessed at www.gao.gov/assets/gao-18-258.pdf on March 1, 2022.

Vaughn, M. (2018). Making sense of student agency in the early grades. *Phi Delta Kappan, 99*(7), 62–66.

Visible Learning. (n.d.). *Collective teacher efficacy (CTE) according to John Hattie.* Accessed at https://visible-learning.org/2018/03/collective-teacher-efficacy-hattie/ on March 27, 2023.

Visible Learning. (2017.) *Visible Learning Plus 250+ influences on student achievement.* Thousand Oaks, CA: Corwin. Accessed at https://visible-learning.org/wp-content/uploads /2018/03/250-Influences-Final-Effect-Size-List-2017_VLPLUS.pdf on June 27, 2023.

Waldman, A. (1999, August 21). Why nobody likes a loser; Failure? No, a bump on the road to success. *The New York Times.* Accessed at www.nytimes.com/1999/08/21/arts/why-nobody -likes-a-loser-failure-no-a-bump-on-the-road-to-success.html on July 15, 2021.

Walker, Tim. (2021, June 17). *Educators ready for fall, but a teacher shortage looms.* National Education Association. Accessed at www.nea.org/advocating-for-change/new-from-nea /educators-ready-fall-teacher-shortage-looms on June 16, 2023.

Wynne, S. P. (2013, January 14). *Zero-tolerance policies in U.S. schools are ineffective and unaffordable.* Accessed at https://jjie.org/2013/01/14/zerotolerance-policies-schools -ineffective-unaffordable-2 on June 16, 2023.

Wehner, R. (2022). *Purpose learning: Reimagining what and how students learn.* National Association of Independent Schools. Accessed at www.nais.org/magazine/independent -school/winter-2022/purpose-learning-reimagining-what-and-how-students-learn/ on March 27, 2023.

Weinberg, M. K., & Tronick, E. Z. (1996). Infant affective reactions to the resumption of maternal interaction after the still-face. *Child Development, 67*(3), 905–914. https://doi .org/10.2307/1131869

Wheaton, A. G., Jones, S. E., Cooper, A. C., & Croft, J. B. (2018, January 26). Short sleep duration among middle school and high school students—United States, 2018. Washington, DC: Centers for Disease Control and Prevention. Accessed at www.cdc.gov/mmwr/volumes /67/wr/pdfs/mm6703a1-H.pdf on March 27, 2023.

Whitehead, L. A. (1983). Domino "chain reaction." American Journal of Physics, 51(2), 182. Accessed at https://popperfont.files.wordpress.com/2013/01/dominopaper.pdf on July 7, 2022.

Yeager, D. S., Henderson, M. D., Paunesku, D., Walton, G. M., D'Mello, S., Spitzer, B. J. et al. (2014). Boring but important: A self-transcendent purpose for learning fosters academic self-regulation. *Journal of Personality and Social Psychology, 107*(4), 559–580. https://doi.org/10 .1037/a0037637

Index

Embracing Relational Teaching
Anthony R. Reibel

When you shift to relational pedagogy, you establish connections that help students feel valued, respected, and heard, which leads to enhanced student engagement. This book explores the relational approach and offers strategies to embed student-teacher relationships into everyday interactions and learning.

BKF949

Parentships in a PLC at Work®
Kyle Palmer

Kyle Palmer draws from his experience as both principal of a model PLC school and as a parent to offer practical strategies for including parents or guardians as part of your collaborative culture focused on student learning.

BKG021

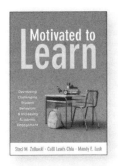

Motivated to Learn
Staci M. Zolkoski, Calli Lewis Chiu, and Mandy E. Lusk

Classroom management can be a challenge without the right skills. With the straightforward strategies gained from *Motivated to Learn*, motivate and engage your students to actively participate in learning while equipping them to better focus in the classroom.

BKG037

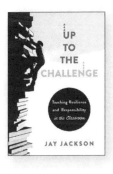

Up to the Challenge
Jay Jackson

This timely resource lets educators take a deep dive into helping students build character to confront and overcome challenges. With passion and purpose, author Jay Jackson blends personal challenges and achievements to equip teachers with tools to improve student resilience.

BKG076

"Tremendous, tremendous, tremendous!

The speaker made me do some very deep internal reflection about the **PLC process** and the personal responsibility I have in making the school improvement process work **for ALL kids.**"

—Marc Rodriguez, teacher effectiveness coach,
Denver Public Schools, Colorado

PD Services

Our experts draw from decades of research and their own experiences to bring you practical strategies for building and sustaining a high-performing PLC. You can choose from a range of customizable services, from a one-day overview to a multiyear process.

Book your PLC PD today!
888.763.9045

Solution Tree